6.95

Prayer Pilgrimage Through Scripture

Rea McDonnell, S.S.N.D.

Prayer Pilgrimage
Through Scripture

Paulist Press
New York / Ramsey

Photo Credits

Chapter	1	Mia et Klaus
Chapter	2	Vivienne della Grotta
Chapter	3	Margarite Hoefler
Chapter	4	Vivienne della Grotta
Chapter	5	Thomas Ackerson
Chapter	6	Mia et Klaus
Chapter	8	Vernon Sigl
Chapter	9	Mia et Klaus
Chapter	10	Paul M. Schrock

Library of Congress
Catalog Card Number: 83-82025

ISBN: 0-8091-2601-X

Published by Paulist Press,
545 Island Road, Ramsey, N.J. 07446

Printed and bound in the United States of America

Contents

Dedicated to the

School Sisters of Notre Dame

in celebration of their 150 years of service

Introduction

After years of teaching biblical spirituality in Boston, grateful to my students who have honed my ideas, I hope with this small book to help Catholic Christians make the word of God their home. Jesus, according to John's Gospel, wants us to be at home in his word so that we can learn from him, be his disciples. Then we will know the truth, and the truth will set us free. That is God's ultimate design for us all: freedom. "If you make my word your home, you will be my disciples. You will know the truth and the truth will set you free" (Jn 8:32).

My second purpose in writing is to deepen our knowledge of Jesus Christ and the one who sent him. This is eternal life, "to know you the one true God and the one whom you have sent" (Jn 17:1–3). Like Paul, all I want for us as we study and pray and share these Scriptures "is to know Christ Jesus and the power of his resurrection" (Phil 3:10). My hope is that this book stirs up our desire, our wanting to know Christ Jesus. I hope that this book stirs up the power of Jesus' resurrection—the power we call Spirit in the hearts and in the communities of us all.

The first chapter of this book explores the value of our using Scripture for a deepening relationship with the Lord. Then I move into the Scriptures themselves. After an introduction to each chapter on, for example, Jewish leaders or

1

psalms or the Gospel of John, I present the heart of the chapter: a selection of Scripture passages to read, study, pray and share. Brief comments on each specific passage and questions guide the reader's remembering and praying these Scriptures. Next, in each chapter, I suggest exercises to help embody the biblical understandings and experiences. These are best shared in a family or group of adults. Finally I suggest further readings.

Special gratitude to my friend Nancy Steckel who prepared the manuscript and who, with her husband John, offered both support and suggestions. I am also grateful to all who have shaped my praying and living the Scriptures, especially Mary Irving, S.S.N.D., Margred Ulmer, S.S.N.D., Rachel Callahan, C.S.C., and Bob Doherty, S.J. Thanks also to Lori Routhier, F.C.S.C.J., my student at the Center for Educational and Pastoral Ministry, Emmanuel College, Boston, who initiated this project and helped with the final typing.

The Word of God

1. The Word of God

We have all heard that Bibles in the Middle Ages were found only in churches, chained to lecterns, that the Scriptures were read only in Latin, and that even in this century Pius X excommunicated Catholic priests who seemed to stray too far afield in their scriptural studies. Yet, in this century, in 1943, Pius XII in his encyclical *Divino Afflante Spiritu* urged Roman Catholics to work with Protestant scholars. We were encouraged to apply critical methods to uncover the texts, the theology, the situations in the life of the biblical authors and their communities from which the Scriptures arose.

Even with this renewed interest in Scripture, you and I were most likely taught in grade and in high school, not with the Scriptures themselves, but Bible stories. I have heard some adult Catholics rail against this shortened form of learning. Nevertheless, these Bible stories communicated something of God's power and saving love. Stories told by Jewish and Christian folk were the very substance from which our own Jewish Scriptures and New Testament took root. Because the early Christians knew the stories of their Jewish ancestors, they were able to apply the Jewish Scriptures to their own daily living and to the life of Jesus himself. Like many peoples, they knew that storytelling is an important means of communicating truth. The story tells more than the literal truth. It carries overtones and undercurrents of emotion, of meaning, of action. Stories can capture the heart of the listener and introduce the hearer to mystery. Whatever we do in the remainder of this book, let us always approach these Scriptures, these stories of God in relationship with us, with a sense of awe, a sense of mystery.

A major shift in Catholic spirituality (that is, the life of the spirit in the community) since Vatican II has moved us away from an individualized private salvation derived from private prayer, private devotions, private reception of the sacraments. Instead of looking to heaven for Jesus or God, we began to experience God or Jesus on earth, not only in worship but also in the interaction of the community. Through that important shift in our understanding and practice of spirituality we were already becoming a biblically formed people. Biblical people are above all community people, those who can recognize God at work not only in their individual lives but also in their community life.

Another important shift in our post-Vatican spirituality has been our experience that God takes the initiative in all spiritual development. In the past we took much initiative, we used self-control and will power, we made sacrifices and we earned merit. We were working our way to heaven and God would bless us with a final seal of approval once we had done all we should. How then have we come to place such great emphasis on God's initiative in our salvation?

I believe that it is through Scripture study that we have come to know these two basic principles: we are a people, and God takes the initiative in fashioning us as his own. In Latin America, where the bishops put the Scriptures in the hands of the ordinary folk long ago, many people are experiencing an immense renewal of faith in Christ, experiencing trust in one another as Christ's new community. As we too in North America begin to read, study, talk about, and pray with the Scriptures we can hope for a rich renewal of the life of the Spirit. Let us look then, first, at the God who takes initiative.

God's Initiative

Our God is one who wants to be known. He reveals himself on the pages of Scripture through the prophets, through the psalmists, through the stories of encounters with Adam and Abraham, through wrestling with Jacob and arguing with Moses. God continues to reveal himself through Jesus and the Spirit, through our prayer and through our history. God is one who still reaches out to lure his people into union with him.

God reveals himself through prayer. When Abraham begs God to spare Sodom and Gomorrah, when Moses pleads for his people with his arms outstretched, when Hannah weeps so bitterly over her barrenness that her prayer seems like drunken murmuring, God reveals himself. God shows himself as one whose face is turned toward them in need, whose heart is devoted to their welfare. He reveals himself as a God whose chief characteristics are *hesed* and *emet*. These two Hebrew terms are untranslatable. The various English translations indicate the rich depths of those words: everlasting love, tender mercy, covenant love, unconditional love, love which endures forever, faithful love, unfailing mercy, etc. The people experience God's steadfast love and devotion, experience God's *hesed* and *emet* not only through their prayer but also through their keen observation of God at work in their human history.

God reveals himself through history, the history of a particular people. Although the Israelites told stories of some individual leaders and founding ancestors, their experience of

God was that he worked with a people. God was active in history: choosing a people, freeing a people, saving a people, leading a people, scolding a people, punishing a people, forgiving a people, haranguing a people, delighting a people, prospering a people. Whatever the event of history, whatever the movement of geography, whatever the political fortunes or failures, people of faith could see God at work in Israel.

Scripture as Sacrament

If God reveals himself through the pages of Scripture, through the stories of his people, through the history of his community, then we who read and digest and incorporate his revealing word are deeply encountering our God who wants so much to be known. We might even say that because of this encounter, Scripture itself is a sacrament. For a long time we have known that sacraments are outward signs designed to give grace. Scripture is certainly an outward sign, something we can hear and see and read and touch and sing. Does Scripture "give grace"? What is grace but the life of God? In Scripture we have an external sign of God communicating himself, his life. Scripture brings us to communion with him, leads us into his very life through our reading, our studying, our praying, our sharing Scripture.

Sacraments do what they signify. The bread of heaven feeds us, the anointing with oil heals us. This word of God, Scripture, does what it signifies: "The word that goes forth from my mouth does not return to me empty but carries out my will and succeeds in doing that for which it was sent" (Is 55:11). Scripture does what it says. For example, when we read in the New Testament about Jesus healing the man born blind (Jn 9), the risen Lord here and now is giving *us* light. He is here and now healing blindness in us. As we read those words of healing and become involved with the word we are participating in the risen Christ's light-giving activity right now. Whether we are sitting quietly in the back of church, working in the yard, or driving the car, Jesus is always in the process of giving us light. This encounter is union with the light-giving Lord. This encounter is possible because we are in contact with the word of God which does what it symbolizes.

If we are reading about the multiplication of the loaves, that story nourishes us. If we are reading the story of the foot washing, Jesus' action for his disciples is his footwashing action right now for us. If we read the story of the paralytic let down through the roof, we are at this moment being brought (in our paralysis) to Jesus for new freedom, new movement. To read Scripture then is to encounter Christ, to let him act in our history. Scripture is an outward sign which brings us into union with God, his Son and Spirit, and thus gives grace.

The early Christians, of course, saw and heard and touched with their hands this word of God, Jesus (1 Jn 1:1). They experienced Jesus in the flesh. They experienced not only his life but his dying and rising. It is that dying and rising of Jesus which is the very core of the New Testament. After their experience the disciples reflected on that experience and then moved into action, to proclaim the good news, to carry on the mission and ministry of Jesus, to articulate the stories of his life and their life. These stories eventually became our Scriptures, the New Testament. We will look at the first disciples' experience, their reflection, and their action throughout the pages of this book. We want to do that only so that our action and our reflection may lead us to an ever deepening experience of God himself, the God who is constantly trying to communicate himself to us.

"This is eternal life: to know you, the one true God." For the Greeks the word "know" means to contemplate, to stand back in order to peer through the eyelashes in order to penetrate the underlying realities. For the Jews, to "know" signifies union, intimate contact, experience. It is through Jesus, the word of God, that we can contemplate, experience, know God. "You will know that I am in my Father, you are in me, and I am in you." When we hear this word, read this word, know this word, our knowledge that God is in us and we in him. has passed from knowledge of our union into actual union. The word of God does what it says.

There are days when we can read a few lines of Scripture and move to affective prayer, to effective ministry or to silent union. There are other days when the pavement has been hard, the bus ride interminable, the students difficult, the patients quarrelsome, the baby screaming with colic. Spontaneous praise or petition just cannot arise through the headache, the bleary eyes, the aching back, the short temper. A passage of Scripture leads only to sleep, or to that kind of nothingness which evokes a nagging guilt that one is really not praying at all. At such times God sends his word to us, a word which will not return empty but which will do what it says. This word will nourish us, cleanse us, free us, heal us, light up our dark places, plunge us into union with God. To spend a time of prayer simply reading Scripture is, in itself, prayer. It is the word of God which accomplishes this prayer and praise and returns fruitful, having done that for which it was sent, having united us with God.

For Further Reading

Ahern, Barnabas. *New Horizons: Studies in Biblical Theology*. Fides Publishers, Inc.: Notre Dame, Indiana, 1963.

Hauser, Richard. *In His Spirit: A Guide to Today's Spirituality*. Paulist Press: New York, 1982.

LaVerdiere, Eugene. *Trumpets of Beaten Metal.* Collegeville, Minn.: Liturgical Press, 1974.

Stuhlmueller, Carroll. *Thirsting for the Lord: Essays in Biblical Spirituality.* New York: Alba House, 1977.

Images of God

2. Images of God

At the core of Jewish religion is the First Commandment of the Decalogue: "I am the Lord your God. You shall not have strange gods before me." To protect themselves from all types of idols, from golden calf to decorative murals, all images of God were forbidden. Yet to communicate their experience of God, the Israelite authors of Scripture sought verbal images to express their understanding of God and his activity on behalf of his people. They imaged him as shepherd, king, rock, dew, warrior, husband, companion, and more. At first, in their more primitive religious experience, the Israelites knew their God to be God of gods, king of the heavenly court of many gods, obviously highest of all gods because he is a God who does justice (Ps 82).

God Is More Than We Can Say

These writers, expressing the faith of the people, knew God as personal, even called him a person. They searched their human experience and saw human beings as the crown of creation (Ps 8). Therefore God must be a person, the highest compliment they could pay. Yet we know that all language about God is analogy. God is not a person. God is more than a person. There is no language which can express who God is in himself. Thus, for me just to have written "himself" is only a minuscule part of the truth of who God really is. God is neither masculine nor feminine. There can be no definition of God because to define means, literally from its Latin root, to set limits. The mystery of who God is goes far beyond our language. The Jewish people dare not even speak his name, YHWH.

Nevertheless, our biblical authors assure us that God continually tries to reveal himself in our human experiences of life, loyalty, war, and work. "In many and various ways God spoke of old to our ancestors . . ." (Heb 1:1). To describe those many and various ways, the authors used verbal images of God throughout the books of Scripture. They were aware of the limits which language imposed on them. God is a rock (Ps 40) but how much more than a rock. God is dew (Hos 14:5) but how much more than dew.

Perhaps, before Jesus, the deepest way his people experienced God was not in thunder and fire or even gentle breezes (1Kgs 19:11–14). They knew God in their most intimate moments of human love. Our first human love is directed to our parents. Thus we find that God is called Father (for example, Jer 3:4) and imaged as mother (not too often, but in Is 49:14–15 and 66:13). As adults, our love turns to courtship with all its joy of being wanted, chosen, with its exquisite emotions of tenderness, despair at separation, longing, ecstacy. The Song of Songs captures in allegory that type of love between God and his beloved Israel. Our adult love, however, so vulnerable and trusting, can be betrayed. Through the experience of the prophet Hosea's broken marriage (Hos 1–3), God tries to communicate how painful is Israel's scorning of his faithful love (*hesed* and *emet*). Human love is often the model and instrument of God's tender fidelity.

Notice that characteristic of our God is his loving, faithful relationship. He is always described in the Scriptures as "for us." Rather than offering philosophical definitions of supreme being, uncaused cause, omnipotent and omniscient, our authors describe God not so much as a being but as a doer. He acts, and acts always on our behalf. His "rockness" is steady for us to cling to, his "dewiness" is gentle to cause our growth, his shepherding is toward pastures to nourish us with abundance, his warring is to protect us from enemies on every side. If we are not fundamentalists, we know that God's portrayal as warrior or father is not absolute truth. Our human experience of God cries out for words to express God. The best we can say is that God is like a warrior on the side of justice, like a father to Jesus and to us. God, to the Israelites, to Jesus, and to some of us, is also like a mother. God is greater than, more than either parent or both parents together. God is more than father, mother, everyone and everything. We call God parent or warrior or gentle dew or steady rock only by analogy.

When we come to images of God as warrior, or even as furious with his chosen people, many of us cringe. How can the God of peace sanction war, let alone lead his people to battle? We must remember that in Scripture we have stories of people's faith experience, not definitions of God's person and nature. Since the Israelites needed to fight defensively and sometimes wanted to fight offensively, since their entire life was permeated by their relationship with God, it was natural for them to find God in their camps, their citadels. They "put not [their] trust in horses," in battle (Ps 33), but only in God whom they believed they honored by their battles. After all, Popes led Crusades in what we like to call more civilized times. Priests and Catholic people in this country celebrated Masses of thanksgiving when the United States bombed Japan not many years ago.

God and Anger

What of God's anger, sometimes depicted in the Jewish
Scriptures as relentless fury? If we believe God is imaged most
perfectly as a real person in a real relationship, then we must
admit that in real relationships anger will always have a
relatively important role. It may be that we have terrifying
experiences of another's anger directed at us. The deeper the
relationship with that person, the deeper the terror, it seems.
Because our Christian spirituality emphasizes the image of
God as father (or even mother) and because most of us were
terrified by our parents' anger with us (cf. *Denial of Death* by
Ernst Becker) we can project that kind of anger onto God. We
may, in reading of God's anger, relive that kind of fear which
stems from our profound helplessness as our parent towers
over us. Even the best, the kindest of parents "towers" over
the naughty child.

It is helpful, as "Christians come of age" (Dietrich Bon-
hoeffer), Christians in adult relationships, to remember our
most loving, deep adult relationship. How is anger expressed
in that relationship? How do you prefer to have this dearest
person's anger expressed to you? What happens after the
storm is spent? What does the relationship look like a week
later? For Jews and for Christians alike, it is important to
express all our emotions in prayer. We often feel angry with
God, with his interference in our life and plans. Anger in a
real and a healthy relationship cannot be expressed only by
one party. Our reading about God's anger in Scripture can
sensitize us to his anger in our relationship with him. As with
a faithful, loving friend or spouse we can hear God's anger,
receive it, repent, cooperate as he transforms us. God's anger
will not destroy us. He too repents of his anger (Am 7:1–6). If
once he chastised us, now he heals (Hos 6:1); if once he
abandoned us in fury, now he names us beloved forever (Is

54:6–10). In healthy human relationships anger expresses intimacy and trust.

New Testament Images

In the New Testament, Jesus offers us other intimate images of God. His unique contribution to our understanding of God may be his calling God "Abba." The Jewish people knew God to be Father, but the intimate "Abba" is Jesus' expression of total trust and vulnerability in relationship. In Mark's portrayal of the agony in the garden, Jesus, tortured by fear, cries "Abba," the equivalent of "Daddy." Paul uses the name twice as he teaches us that the Spirit of the risen Jesus is deep in our innermost being, crying "Abba" (Gal 4:6, Rom 8:15). It seems that the ultimate expression of our relationship with God is "Abba"—a word which we cannot appropriate to ourselves but which is completely dependent on the Spirit's gift, the Spirit's prayer within us.

Two other images of God which Jesus offers us express God's *hesed*, his passionate devotion to us. Jesus calls God a shepherd, an image not unknown to the psalmists (Pss 23 and 80) nor to the prophets (Ez 34). What may be special to Jesus' own century, however, is the disdain of the people for shepherds. According to Joachim Jeremias in *Jerusalem in the Time of Jesus*, all shepherds were considered guilty of thieving by reason of their profession. In Luke 15:1–10 then, when Jesus likens his Father to a good shepherd, he underscores his Father's devotion to the sinner, the maligned, the outcast. Luke adds an intimate touch to the story found in Matthew 18:12–14: the shepherd in Luke lifts the lost sheep to his shoulder and carries it. Immediately following the image of God as shepherd Luke's Gospel offers another image showing God aligned with the most outcast group in the Jewish community: women. "If a woman has ten silver pieces and loses one of them . . ." God searching for his lost people is like a woman searching for her coin.

Jesus, Image of God

Whether we search the Jewish Scriptures or the New Testament we discover images of God expressive of human longing to see the face of God, to hear his voice, savor his taste. All these human expressions fall short. But, as in any relationship, the lover wants to reveal himself or herself to the beloved. So we are not dependent on merely human strivings to know God, human searches to understand the Lord. Once again God takes the initiative and reveals himself in the perfect image, communicates his most inner life in a perfect expression of himself. We call that perfect image "Jesus." As the author of Hebrews phrases it, Jesus is "the express image of God's person" (1:3). Paul directly calls Jesus the image of God, but John the evangelist portrays the entire human history of the Word as Jesus' imaging his Father. Jesus does and works and says only as he sees the Father doing and working, only what he hears the Father saying. "If anyone sees me, Philip, he sees the Father" (Jn 14:9).

All verbal images, all words fall silent in the presence of the Word of God, Jesus, who completely expresses what God is, who God is, God's loves and hates, God's desires and angers. This is not to relegate Jesus to the car's dashboard as "good old plastic Jesus," so perfect that he cannot be human, God in a thin disguise. That is the scandal, that is the glory of the incarnation. Our God wanted to be immersed in flesh, *sarx*, the Greek word for butcher meat. The Word became *sarx*. As *sarx*, Jesus grew in wisdom and age and grace, becoming ever more human, ever more expressing God's life within him. Jesus worked through all the developmental stages we work through, had his cranky days, and days when he flowed in total "sync" with life, was affected by seasons and sunshine, moods and mysteries until he became so fully human that he pioneered the promise to humanity: we all are made in the image of God. In Jesus the potential gradually became reality.

Guided Prayer

I suggest you take only one of the following passages a day so that during the day your mind and heart might return to the passage, to the God revealed in the passage. The guiding material may not help you pray. I suggest you read the Scripture passage without looking at the guiding notes and follow your own intuitions, feelings, movements of the heart. When the passage "dries up" for you, try the guiding material.

Psalm 68. Focus on verses 1-10 and 19-20:
"He bears our burdens, day after day. Our God is a God who saves." Now his freeing, dignifying, protecting action is brought closer to home; we are lonely, imprisoned; we are a worn-out land; we are poor. Give him your burdens to bear. Show him where in your life you feel oppressed, helpless, injured, poor. Change the "he" to "you," and address God personally.

Psalm 146:
The Israelites did not define God as being; they related to him as a doer, and primarily a doer of justice for the poor and oppressed. Notice how the Lord acts in this psalm. Then reread it, changing the "he" to "you." Address God person-

ally. Ask him to reveal to you just when in your lifetime he has done these freeing, dignifying, protecting things . . . for you, for the world.

Hosea. Read Chapters 1–3; return to Hosea 2:19:

God is imaged as husband and lover. "I will betroth you with unfailing devotion and love," the Lord says. Tell him how you would like him to be devoted to you, how you would like him to love you. Listen to how *he* wants to show you love and devotion.

Isaiah 35:

God is a gardener. When has the Lord strengthened and steadied you, opened your eyes and your ears, made your dry places a lush garden? Thank him for his goodness in your life.

Job 38:1–5:

Join Job as he stands in awe before the mystery of God. God questions Job into a new realization of who human beings are and who God is. Ponder with the psalmist: "What are persons that you should be mindful of them?" What does God so love about our humanity that he sent his Son? How do you feel about his nearness—and his otherness? Share those feelings with him.

Genesis 32:3–12; 33:1–16:

What parable of Jesus does this story remind you of? How is God imaged here? Talk with the Lord about relationships in which you have failed, about which you are afraid. Then remember and discuss with him those people who have been kind to you, have "gone at your pace," and so have opened your capacity for deeper relationship.

Genesis 32:24–31:

God is a wrestler. An intimate relationship may entail wrestling with the Lord, or receiving a new name. Remember and talk with the Lord about the times you have wrestled with him. Show him your wounds in all your relationships, how you are still hurting, still "limping." Ask for healing.

Genesis 3:21:

Tailors in other times were men. In our culture, women are usually the ones who sew. God is imaged as a seamstress here, sewing tunics for the shamed Adam and Eve. How do you feel about the image of God as feminine? How do you feel about God's painstaking work envisioned here (remember how in ancient times needles were clumsy bits of bone, thread usually strips of animal skin). What do you learn about God from picturing him as a seamstress? Share your feelings with him.

How To Share Faith

Obviously these passages can be used by oneself. A more fruitful way to use them is to gather in a weekly group meeting for faith sharing. Faith sharing presupposes that you are trying to pray with Scripture regularly. You would meet to share with others how "the word has found a home" in you, how God is working in your own story as you dialogue with his story.

In faith sharing I suggest a discipline at which my students have often balked but which "works" to the group's advantage eventually. I suggest that as a person speaks about a Scripture passage and how he or she is challenged or comforted, what memories, desires, feelings it stirred, no one say a word in response. We are tempted to compare the speaker's journey to our own, we are anxious to assure the timid that we understand, we are quick to make judgments about the speaker's content. Judgments must be set aside— judgments about truth and falsehood because a person's experience with God is true, uniquely true to him or her; judgments about maturity and immaturity because a person's human and spiritual development is his or her unique pilgrimage to God; judgments about the beauty, the depth, the giftedness of the faith experience because of insidious comparisons that we make with our own experience's beauty and depth (usually falling far short of the other's), because of temptations for the group to play the game of impressing one another.

After a few meetings my students realize what advantages the discipline of not responding verbally can offer. First, no judgments can be expressed and so the private judgments eventually grow less persistent. My students experience themselves as open to receive whatever the speaker will share. Some find God quite present in their own receptivity as they mirror God's own receptivity to the speaker. Second, they realize that they are contemplating. Very simply, contemplation means noticing with such total absorption that one's self is forgotten. Music, oceans, sunsets, a baby's fingers can "catch" us in contemplation. Not preparing a verbal response, my students find that they are completely absorbed both in the other person and in God's revealing of himself in the other's story of faith. They realize that as their listening skills are sharpened, their communication skills are broadened; accustomed to verbalizing, they discover that eyes, smiles, faces, and postures communicate effectively. The medium of faith-sharing, the process itself, becomes a message of openness, contemplation, listening to the word and responding with one's body.

Some will prefer a global sharing on all the images of God passages; others may share on just one passage that touched them. I would suggest that after each person has a chance to share, the group end with some quiet absorption time together. The group might decide to hold hands during the silent time. Someone might create a prayer to conclude with, or the Our Father or a hymn might end the meeting. If a group of six meets only for thirty minutes in the beginning, be patient. As group members grow in trust the meetings may lengthen. At the beginning of the group it might be wise to agree on some ground rules about regular attendance, confidentiality, a maximum time limit, monopolizing, etc. Every two or three meetings a rotating chairperson could call for a fifteen minute evaluation of the group's process according to the original ground rules.

"Where two or three are gathered together" in Jesus' name, Jesus is present, revealing God's faithful love for us. We too are instruments of God's respect and care for each of us as we move together on pilgrimage through the Scriptures.

Exercises

■ Let your imagination run free. In how many and in what various ways can you describe God—for you? For example, could God be a bed, cool water on a hot day, a warm fire during winter's storms?

■ We may not have much experience of shepherds. Who in our society takes care of the helpless? Reflect.

■ High school teachers often challenge youngsters to rewrite the psalms. One teen on probation wrote, paraphrasing Psalm 23: "The Lord is my case worker. No reason to run scared." Rewrite your favorite psalm—for you.

■ Try to dance your image of God. Draw God. Write a haiku poem of three lines, using two syllables, five syllables, two syllables per line to describe God.

■ What image of you does God prefer? Try to "get inside his skin" and look at yourself. Are you, for him, a shepherd, a rock, thunder, dew? What name does God call you?

Can you find a group with whom to share your images, your rewritten psalm, your dance, your drawing? It may be different from your faith-sharing group. It may be your family. After a group has worked through the exercises in this book each member could form his or her own group and walk through the "Pilgrimage" again. One of the beauties of this *living* word is that a month, a year later, we can come fresh to the word which will speak to us in new situations, new relationships.

For Further Reading

Brown, Raymond E. *Jesus, God and Man: Modern Biblical Reflections*. Milwaukee: Bruce, 1967.
Jesus is the ultimate expression of God. Somewhat difficult but worth the mental discipline. The topic is itself difficult.

Hart, Thomas. *The Art of Christian Listening*. New York: Paulist Press, 1980.
A must for those in faith-sharing groups. Practical.

Phillips, J.B. *Your God Is Too Small*. New York: Macmillan, 1961.

An essay on images of God.

The Leaders

3. The Leaders

Much of the Jewish Scripture is devoted to its heroes and heroines and how they related with God. God's initiative in these relationships usually took the form of a call, a vocation to leadership or prophecy. Like ourselves, these men and women had to trust that the call was no delusion, had to risk, usually beginning a pilgrimage over uncharted waters. In this chapter we will focus on some called to leadership in Israel: Abraham, Joseph, Moses, Joshua, Gideon, Samuel, David and Solomon. I will briefly describe these leaders in chronological order and their contribution. My purpose, like the authors' of these stories, is not to present historical material, but to show God's unfailing care for his people. I keep my commentary brief so that the Scripture passages in the Guided Prayer section may speak for themselves. I will conclude by reflecting on some overarching themes: God's choice of the weak, covenant, sin, liberation, and law.

Sketches of Israel's Leaders

Abraham is called patriarch, father of the chosen people. He is introduced abruptly in Genesis 12, under command by the Lord to leave country and family in order to explore new land. God promises a blessing, promises that Abraham's name itself shall be a blessing. Since blessing is a share in the life of the blessing one, Abraham is above all called to share God's life. God's life is fruitful, and Abraham's line begins with the birth of Isaac (Gen 21).

Isaac's grandson Joseph interpreted dreams, a kind of call to be God's spokesperson (Gen 40–41). As redeemer of his family from famine, Joseph became the hero of Israel, noted for his forgiveness of the very brothers who sold him into Egyptian slavery. As his brothers pleaded with him, now a royal official in Egypt dispensing food, "Joseph could no longer control his feelings. . . . Joseph made himself known to his brothers and so loudly did he weep" that his attendants heard him. Joseph repeated to his brothers that God sent him ahead to Egypt to save lives from famine. Then "he kissed all his brothers and wept over them" (Gen 45).

In Egypt for some four hundred years, the Israelites became slaves there. Moses, saved from death as an infant, struck an Egyptian dead in fury over injustice meted out to Hebrew slaves. From the desert where Moses was hiding for many years, God's call reached him. He was to lead his people to freedom. Uncertain, Moses responded, "But they will never believe me or listen to me. They will say, 'The Lord did not appear to you' " (Ex 4:1). Of course God prevailed in this verbal wrestling match with the man who was to become Israel's greatest leader and friend of God. "There has never yet risen in Israel a prophet like Moses whom the Lord knew face to face" (Dt 34:10).

Moses was succeeded by Joshua, warrior and confidant of Moses. In Deuteronomy 31:14 the Lord says to Moses, "Call Joshua and then come and stand in the tent of the presence so that I may give him his commission." Before Moses died he laid hands on Joshua; at that point Joshua was filled with the spirit of wisdom. Not only did he lead the people into the promised land, but he acted as their spiritual leader as well.

Historically it seems that after taking possession of the land, the tribes of Israel, not really united, were governed by judges noted for wisdom and warring skills. When one of the twelve tribes was attacked, some of the neighboring tribes might join the battle, as in the case of the judge Deborah (Jgs 4). Basically the "raising up" of judges was the Lord's work. The Spirit of the Lord would "wrap the judge round" (Knox translation), inspiring leadership for crisis stiuations.

When Gideon is called to be a judge, he argues with the Lord, pleading that his clan is the weakest in his tribe, that he is the least in his family (Jgs 6:15). After spectacular victory, the people beg Gideon to stay on as their ruler. He insists that only the Lord is ruler of Israel, but later is tempted to power and idolatry (Jgs 8:22–27).

The last judge of Israel is the majestic Samuel, circuit rider dispensing justice and speaking on behalf of God. Samuel's vocation is the familiar call of the boy in the middle of the night. "Speak, Lord, your servant is listening" (1 Sam 3:10–11) is the child's response. An older Samuel struggled with his people who wanted a king, a permanent ruler over Israel. The Lord told Samuel how rejected he felt by this people whom he had led out of Egypt, and he warned them of the troubles a king would bring, but they still wanted a king and the Lord gave them Saul. When Samuel approached Saul, the young man protested that his was the smallest tribe, his family the least important in the tribe (1 Sam 9:21). After Samuel anointed Saul "God gave Saul a new heart" (1 Sam 10:10).

Saul's fortunes, despite the new God-given heart, were tied to war. Once, disobedient to the Lord's command, Saul was warned by Samuel: "You have rejected the word of the Lord and therefore the Lord has rejected you as king over

Israel'' (1 Sam 15:26). While Saul was still in power, Samuel anointed David, the youngest of a family of sons. Saul's mental disturbances were soothed when the boy David played his harp. Soon the youth became both a threat to the insecure king and a friend to the king's son Jonathan (1 Sam 18–20).

When David ascended the throne he united the twelve tribes around not only his new capital city, Jerusalem, but also the ark of the covenant which had been captured by the Philistines and recovered by David. So great was the king's joy that he danced before the ark as it processed through the Judean hills toward Jerusalem (2 Sam 6:12–23). A new promise was given David and his descendants through the prophet Nathan (2 Sam 7:8–16), the same Nathan who would later accuse the king of sinning by usurping power which belongs only to the Lord. David however was beloved of the Lord before and after his great sin of adultery with Bathsheba and the murder of her husband to cover up his sin (2 Sam 11—12).

David's son Solomon abused power. Injustice, slavery, and murder reigned in the wealthy court of Solomon. Materialism prevailed and God was spurned. After Solomon's death the kingdom was split, with the northern ten tribes taking the name Israel, the southern two tribes becoming known as Judah.

Some Common Experiences of Leaders

From these thumbnail sketches the reader can see some common threads in the lives of Israel's leaders. Their call to leadership often surprised them, and often they protested that they were too weak, too insignificant to do God's work. It is particularly instructive to know that God chose one murderer,

Moses, to lead the exodus from Egypt; another, David, to provide the model of kingship. A number of leaders failed their God: Gideon, Saul, Solomon. God seems to delight in selecting the sinner and the insignificant.

Often these leaders made a covenant with God. Abraham, Moses, and David received promises of the Lord's unswerving fidelity, sealed by a covenant. The great Israelite covenant was the one made at Sinai in which the Lord gave his law to the people through Moses' mediation. *If* you keep my law, I will be your God, the Lord promised. This covenant was conditional.

God rescued his people from Egypt's oppression, "bearing them up on eagles' wings," but they forgot their Redeemer and began to sin. A new oppression would call them to their senses and in their desperation they would cry out to God whose heart would melt. He would save his people once again. He would be their God *if* they would keep his law. How they would promise fidelity when the rescue was still fresh! Throughout the pages of the Jewish Scriptures echoes the refrain: sin/oppression/cry/deliverance.

Deliverance is an important experience of the people. God constantly reminds them of his mighty devotion to them in the exodus experience. They remind each other—in worship, psalms, stories. The exodus is the touchstone against which other manifestations of God are measured. One manifestation of God's faithful presence was the ark of the covenant, fashioned in the desert. It contained the law and later some manna and the rod of Aaron. It was housed in the tabernacle, literally the tent of presence. The Israelites' God was free to pack up his tent and move on pilgrimage with his people.

Another manifestation of God's presence to Israel was the law, the Torah. We are perhaps prejudiced against the Law. Deep currents of legalism and consequent guilt can flood us if we were taught that the Jewish law applied to us Christians. We find Jesus in the Gospels railing against the legalism of the Pharisees. But to the Jew who loved the law, it was life, a reminder of God's covenanting love and constant liberation.

Often the law is linked with the prophets. Prophecy is yet another manifestation of God's presence among his people. Of course some of Israel's leaders were designated prophets: Moses, Deborah, Samuel, even Saul. They were God's spokespersons, calling the people back to covenant, promising God's liberation. We will explore prophecy and the works of some of the prophets in the next chapter.

Guided Prayer

ABRAHAM. Genesis 15:1-8:
Relating with someone means being called to trust, to risk, to change, to journey. Remember your relationships and your growth in trust. On the other hand, when have you felt that all is lost? What comfort or promise have you felt at that time? "Lord, how can I be sure . . . ?" Tell him how you feel.

JOSEPH. Read Genesis 39—45 for background; Pray Psalm 105: 16-24:
Out of slavery comes freedom. Remember some of your sufferings, especially the injustices you have suffered. Discuss them and your feelings about them with the Lord. Ask for his continuing healing and growth in hope that out of death will come life.

MOSES. Read Exodus 33: 17-23; 34: 5-7:
Ask the Lord to reveal himself to you. What does he tell you that his name is? Ask him where in your life *you* can find his face, his glory. Listen to his reply.

Read Exodus 15:19—17:13:

Notice how Moses is a man who is as intimately involved with his people as he is with the Lord. How do you work out the dynamic of action for people and contemplation of the Lord in your own life? Instead of thinking about it, philosophizing about it, ask the Lord to instruct you. How does he want your spiritual life and your family life, your life of ministry to interact?

Reread Exodus 33:17-23:

What are your strongest experiences of the Lord? How do you "see" his face? Rejoice and be grateful. When or where have you seen the "back" of the Lord? What does that mean for you? How do you feel about these experiences? Discuss them with him.

JOSHUA. Joshua 24:1-28:

Notice how before Joshua calls on the people to make a choice (v 15) he calls to their memory the saving actions of Yahweh on their behalf, a sign to them of how God loves them. The people respond and Joshua confronts them (v 19)—you are sinners, he tells them in effect. Only if we really know the Lord's kindness to us have we the courage to admit our sin. Only if we admit it can we repent. But notice that in bringing us to repentance God takes the initiative in reminding us how he has always cared for us. Speak with the Lord about this dynamic of his love/your repentance in your own life.

GIDEON. Read Judges 6—8 for background; Judges 6:12-18:

How do you feel about Gideon's relationship with the Lord? Would you like to be so honest with him? Tell him how you feel, what you want in your relationship with him.

Judges 6:25–34:
Gideon risks in order to follow the Lord's way. Remember the risks, the hard things you have done in order to follow Jesus, even to the cross. Tell him how you feel about these past risks and what you want for the future.

Judges 6:36–40; 7:1–25:
Gideon goes to battle with only three hundred men. Gideon tests the Lord and the Lord tests Gideon. How are you, in the present, testing the Lord and how is he testing you? Tell him how you feel.

DAVID. Read 2 Samuel 11; pray 2 Samuel 12:1–14:
"Had this not been enough, I would have added other favors as great." The Lord reminds David of all the gifts he has given the king. Why, the Lord asks, must David take matters into his own hands? How does our desire to control things, people, our own lives usurp his power? Talk with him about control and surrender, about your creaturehood and his lordship.

Exercises

■ Read more extensively the chapters describing your favorite Israelite leader. What qualities of leadership do you find in him or her? What qualities are needed in Church and political leaders today? Ask members of your group to reflect on their own leadership abilities. Where, when, how does each lead? Discuss. Be open to feedback from the group should they affirm your abilities.

■ In the privacy of your room, remember God's presence and dance for him as David did.

■ Pay attention to all the "shoulds" in your life on any given day. Write the times you acted, thought, felt a certain way because you "should." Where do these "shoulds" come from? Parents, teachers, preachers? The Jewish law? Jesus? What do you want to do with these "shoulds"?

■ Which leader in the Jewish Scriptures do you like best? Why? Which one challenges you most? Why? Share with your group.

■ Old hat perhaps, but try a "trust walk," trying to get inside the skin of Abraham who walked into a strange country. Let someone lead you, blindfolded. Share your feelings with the group.

■ How is it that God seems to sanction war, choose warriors? Discuss.

For Further Reading

Brueggemann, Walter. *Prophetic Imagination.* Philadelphia: Fortress Press, 1978.
A critique of Solomon's court and how the injustices of that century speak to our own materialistic numbness. Perhaps a bit scholarly.

Chayevsky, Paddy. *Gideon.* New York: Dramatist Play Service.
This play, sometimes televised, is a most refreshing portrayal of Gideon's intimate relationship with God. Perhaps one of the best examples of a biblical spirituality is Gideon's.

Twigg, Blanche. *God Calls a People*, Cincinnati: St. Anthony
    Messenger, 1978.
    *A small book for beginners who need an overview of
biblical history, geography, politics. A good tool for adult
education groups.*

The Lovers

4. The Lovers

Prophets speak the word of God to the people. That word, we learn from Hebrews 4:12–13, is a two-edged sword which can penetrate the most hidden motives of our hearts. The word spoken by the prophets cuts to the core of a sinning people, warning, pleading, challenging, critiquing. The other edge of the sword wielded by the prophets is silken soft, a word to soothe a people oppressed by enemies or their own unjust rulers. Prophets comfort or challenge, criticize or console. Prophets do not make specific predictions of the future.

One of the ways Christians used the Jewish Scriptures from the time of Peter's speech on Pentecost was to find in them verification of all God had done in the death and resurrection of Jesus. The Jews believed that anyone who hung on a tree was cursed by God (Dt 21:23), and that therefore Jesus was cursed by God. The first Christians had to "prove" that Jesus was, on the contrary, blessed by God. To prove this they would use the authority of the Jewish Scriptures. Probably one of the most convincing passages is the Suffering Servant song of Isaiah 53. In that passage God lets his loved one suffer but finally vindicates him. It was a short step for Christians to imagine that Isaiah had seen into the future and could predict Jesus' torture and death. To make such an application of a particular Scripture passage to a

43

particular person or situation was a common practice among Jews in Jesus' time. It is still a practice among some Christians who once were certain that parts of the Book of Revelation applied to Kaiser Wilhelm, The Third Reich, communism's rise, etc. The world has not ended, nor is God deceiving us. We are using Scripture for purposes never intended by the authors or by the Spirit when we use it to try to predict the future.·

Prophecy is the voice God has lent to the silent agony of humankind, writes Rabbi Abraham Heschel. Prophets are mightily concerned with justice, with politics, with widows and orphans. Prophecy springs from identification with the suffering of the people. Prophecy is especially the record of the prophets' identifying with the suffering of God. Prophets are so united with God that they share his feelings as well as his mind and his word.

Amos

Amos and Hosea are two prophets who spoke to the northern kingdom of Israel in the decades before that kingdom fell in 721 B.C. Amos is a shepherd who protests his prophetic vocation. Nonetheless he shares God's passion for justice. For Greek philosophers the supreme characteristic of God was apathy—literally *a-pathos*, without passion. Not so for the Jews. Their God was full of passion. God's hatred expressed by Amos (i.e., 5:21; 6:8) shows God's passionate revulsion for pomp, arrogance, religiosity, wealth, trampling on the rights of the defenseless. God's judgment is on those who offend the poor (Am 8) and he roars that judgment like a lion (Am 1:2; 3:8). Amos envisions a rolling river of justice, a powerful image in such an arid land as Israel. This justice which the prophet proclaims so vehemently is not legal so much as communal, springing from covenant relationship. Our injustice is a betrayal of our God who is justice.

Hosea

No prophet understands betrayal so well as Hosea. This prophet marries a woman who is unfaithful. So deep and lasting is his love that he cannot face separation, and so he keeps wooing her back to him, hoping that her fidelity might some day match his own. Hosea's call to prophecy is an inner identification of his love and fidelity, his fury at the injustice of her betrayals, his forgiveness that wipes out the past with God's own *hesed* and *emet*.

Isaiah

The prophecy of Isaiah was compiled over decades. The original prophet Isaiah was an aristocrat from Jerusalem, called in a majestic vision of God. "Whom shall I send?" cries the Lord. Isaiah eagerly replies, "Send me" (Is 6:9). From his prophecy derived a hope for a Messiah from King David's line, an ideal "Prince of Peace." Like other prophets, Isaiah not only uses words to communicate God's messages of promise and doom, but he uses the prophetic gesture, a bodily sign. For three years Isaiah walks naked to symbolize how Assyria would strip the nations naked (Is 20).

Two centuries later, near the end of the Babylonian exile (538 B.C.), more material was added to the prophecy of Isaiah. Chapters 40—55 are called Deutero (or Second) Isaiah. The theology of this prophet focuses on a new age dawning, a new exodus as God delivers his people again from bondage in Babylon. God is known now, not only as Savior, the primal experience of the Israelite community, but also as Creator. Salvation is universal, possible for all nations. Some scholars attribute Chapters 56—66 to Third Isaiah. This material was written after the exile. The prophet focuses on the rebuilding of Jerusalem, the new temple (Is 62:1–7). The day of the Lord, once a frightening threat of God's anger (Am 8:9), becomes a light, a time of ingathering for all peoples. (Is 60).

Jeremiah

The last of the lovers we will treat is Jeremiah. The Book of Jeremiah is the self-disclosure of a passionate lover of his Lord. Living near Jerusalem with his priestly family, Jeremiah experiences his prophetic vocation in 626 B.C. He prophesies right up to the destruction of Jerusalem by the Babylonians. He is to remain celibate as a prophetic sign that chaos will befall the people and their children (16:1–4). For forty-six years Jeremiah was a prophet and he was exhausted. Even God fails him. The prophet laments:

> Why then is my pain unending,
> my wound desperate and incurable?
> You are to me like a brook that is not to be trusted,
> whose waters fail (15:18).

But Jeremiah identifies with God, particularly feeling God's pain (2:5; 14:17), God's homelessness among his own people, in his own land (14:8–9). "I am full of the wrath of God," he asserts (6:11). God's word is like a fire in his heart (20:7–

12), burning him up, burning him out. Not only the length of his career, the intensity of his passions, but constant persecution wears him down. Both mental and physical punishment are his (18:23; Chapters 36 and 38).

Out of Jeremiah's experience with God and people grows the promise of a new covenant (31: 31–34) which God will make with a people of circumcised hearts (4:4). Out of the prophet's experience with one of the very few good kings from David's line, Josiah, comes Jeremiah's belief that to know the Lord is to do justice (22:13–16).

Justice is a chief theme of all these prophetic lovers. When we say that the God of the Old Testament is a God of justice while the God of the New Testament is a God of mercy, we perpetuate an ancient Christian heresy. The God of the Old Testament is a God of mercy. Mercy is often the translation of *hesed* which is most characteristic of the God of Israel. The God of the New Testament is a God of justice. Justice is also most characteristic of Jesus who himself hungers and thirsts for justice (Mt 5:6). Righteousness or holiness is another way, etymologically, to name God's justice. The prophets who preached social justice were receiving their words of justice from the source of all holiness, God. To know the Lord, to be intimately united with him, is for each of us, in our time and political situation, to do God's justice.

Guided Prayer

AMOS. Amos 4:6-13:

The Lord is lamenting, crying out of the deep anger of being betrayed. When have you felt betrayed? Ask the Lord to let you remember the pain of it so that you may feel with him what your sin and mine causes him to "feel."

Amos 7:1-3:
When we feel that God is angry, we tend to cringe. We need to lower our proud heads and admit, "We are so small." Ask him to deal out justice to the small people, ask him to repent of his anger over our hardened hearts.

HOSEA. Read Hosea, Chapters 1—3; Return to 2:7-8:
What are the "corn, new wine and oil" in your life? What good gifts has the Lord lavished on you? Let your gifts just bubble up; don't scrape your memory looking for them. How do you feel about them?

Hosea 6:1-3:
This section is in praise of the Lord's justice. How do you feel about his justice in your life? Discuss that with him. Has he ever torn you and not healed you? Do you *feel* healed? Tell him what you need.

Hosea 6:4-6:
Ask for a gift of steady faithfulness that won't vanish like the morning mist. Ask him that you might trust his faithfulness. Remind him that you want to know him (remember that "knowing" means being attached to) and ask him to know you too.

Hosea 11:1-11:
What lines move you to respond to the Lord's love?

Hosea 14:3-9:
Our God is a father, a healer, a lover, a dew, a sheltering pine tree. Discuss what you have learned about who God is from Hosea. Has this prophet helped you to know—be attached to—the Lord? How do you know him now?

ISAIAH. Read Isaiah 1:10-20; Return to v 17:

Verse 17 is the prophet's conception of true morality; it is Jesus' idea too. Who are the oppressed, the orphans, the widows in your life? What people need you? How do you respond to them? Talk with the Lord about your response. Ask for the gifts of compassion and justice.

Isaiah 43:1-13:

Verse 4 can be translated: I give whole worlds for you. Verse 13 assures you that he holds you, and nothing, no one can snatch you away from his grasp. How do you feel about the message of v 1–13? of v 4? of v 13? Ask him for the gift of trust that you may really believe and rejoice in his love for you.

Isaiah 46:3-5:

Who is like me? the Lord asks. He carries us, he bears our burdens. That is the image of the God with whom Isaiah relates. What is your image of God? Ask him to show you who he is for *you*.

Isaiah 49:8-16:

V 10: One who loves you will lead you. Ask again for trust. Vv 14–15: Have you ever felt forgotten by the Lord? Talk with him about it, even if you feel angry with him. He's big enough to take your anger! Again ask for trust that he will never forget you, that you are unique and special to him.

Isaiah 55:

Read this slowly, for the word of the Lord does what it says: nourishes, calls you back, penetrates, causes rejoicing. What lines make you feel something? Express those feelings to the Lord.

Isaiah 62:1–5:
The word of the Lord does what it says. You *are* being held as precious in the hand of the Lord. You *are* never forsaken. You *are* the Lord's delight, his beloved. You *are* the cause of the Lord's rejoicing, even as this word is spoken to you today. Ask to believe that his word makes all this a reality for you right now. How do you *feel* about what he is doing for you, with you? Share those feelings with him.

JEREMIAH. Jeremiah 1:4–10:
Do you ever argue with the Lord? About what? If not, why not? When you tell him your limitations and he tells you differently, can you hear him? (He may be speaking through your friends who affirm you and your gifts.) Are you afraid to be chosen by the Lord for any further task? Discuss these things with him.

Jeremiah 31:31–34; 32:36–41:
A new covenant is promised. If you could write your own covenant with the Lord, how would you address him? What would he promise you? What name would he call you? How would you feel? Ask him, simply, what he thinks of your desires. Does he inspire you to make any changes in your covenant?

Jeremiah 4:19; 20:7–9; 23:9; 23: 28–30:
Can you, who were chosen as a prophet at your baptism, in any way identify with Jeremiah as he wrestles with his call to speak the word of challenge and comfort? For whom do you speak this word? This is the mission the Lord gives you. How do you feel about it? Discuss these things with the one who puts his word in your mouth.

Jeremiah 8:18—9:1:
Do you feel deeply about people? Which ones? Why? Is anything blocking you from caring more consistently? Can you get angry with those you care about? Feel tenderness? Talk with the Lord about the whole range of feelings in your relationships and ask for the gift of compassion.

Jeremiah 3:12-13; 8:4-6:
How capable are you of admitting your creaturehood, your sinfulness? How capable are you of forgiving yourself your own humanity? How capable is the Lord of forgiving your most gross rebellion? Ask to trust this unconditional love, to trust that he loves you just the way you are.

Jeremiah 30:17; 31:7-14:
How able are you to receive from other people (favors, gifts, assistance at a task, etc.)? How able are you to accept kindness—from others? from the Lord? If you really allow him to heal you and to whole you, what will be different in your life? Talk about these things with him.

Exercises

■ God has given each of us a prophetic vocation through baptism. Remember and share a time when something bigger, someone greater than yourself took over and gave you an appropriate word or gesture of comfort or challenge for someone else, gave you a word to comfort or challenge your family or community.

■ Listen to Handel's "Messiah." Many people are only familiar with the Christmas sections based on Isaiah. If the death/resurrection material moves you, find someone to share it with you.

■ Lovers identify with each other. The prophets identify with God. Remember being in love. Take five minutes of silent remembering in your group. Share the experience, feelings, memories in a faith sharing style. Then take another five minutes of silence together and feel that "in love" experience with God. Conclude without words in the group but with a sign, a hug of peace.

■ Besides the poignant picture of God as passionate, wronged lover, Hosea offers a picture of God as parent, mother or father, teaching a child to walk (Hos 11:3–4). The northern kingdom, called Ephraim here, was called out of Egypt at the exodus. God speaks through the prophet:

> It was I who taught Ephraim to walk,
> I who had taken them in my arms.
> They did not know that I . . . led them with bonds of love,
> that I had lifted them like a little child to my cheek,
> that I had bent down to feed them.

Let two people in the group act out "their" first child's steps. The group watches faces, eyes, body language during the role-play. The imaginary baby falls. How do the "parents" respond? After the role-play let the "parents" report their own feelings, then receive feedback from the group. How do the observers feel? Have any in the group ever felt that, as they learned to walk in Christian life, God was waiting for their first misstep, their first fall, to swoop down on them with hell-fire? Discuss. How can we be healed of that image of God? How can we be instruments of healing for others? Discuss.

■ Many of the words to modern hymns are taken from the prophets. Pay attention to the sources of next Sunday's hymns and share with your group one or two of your favorite hymns based on the prophets.

For Further Reading

Heschel, Abraham. *The Prophets*. New York: Harper & Row, 1962.
A scholarly treatment yet capable of being used for spiritual reading.

Reid, David. *What Are They Saying About the Prophets?* New York: Paulist, 1980.
Delightfully fresh insights, useful for adult education groups.

Stuhlmueller, Carroll. *The Prophets and the Word of God*. Notre Dame, Ind.: Fides, 1966.

The Psalms

5. The Psalms

The word "psalms" means praises. In the one hundred and fifty psalms recorded in our Scriptures, however, we find expressed not only praises but laments, thanks, curses, desires, joys, sufferings. Every emotion is proclaimed to God, every curse and blessing is spoken in his hearing. Psalms are prayers of the heart, acknowledgements that God permeates each of us at the core (Latin: *cor*, heart). He is the source of our intensity and the initiator of our intense relationship with him. Our relationship is expressed in the psalms in a variety of ways.

Scholars classify psalms in a variety of ways, but I suggest certain types of psalms for your personal and group praying. I will begin with the most problematic type, the cursing psalm. The historical psalms offer an excellent way to share faith. Laments, complaining psalms make up one-third of the psalter and deserve our attention; so do psalms of praise and thanksgiving. Scholars also debate whether the psalms are written for communities or for individuals. Because of my overarching belief that Scripture is a community expression of faith, I hold that all psalms are communitarian, even though sometimes cast in the first person and revealing most private sentiments.

Psalms as Poetry

Scholars do agree that psalms are poetry. Hebrew poetry is characterized by parallelism. One of the ways we can understand the meaning of Hebrew words is to pay attention to parallelism. For example, the psalmist prayed:

Bless the Lord, O my soul
And all my being, bless his holy name (Ps 103).

We can diagram the parallelism like this:

Bless the Lord, O my soul

And all my being, bless his holy name.

"Soul" in the first line is in parallel position with "all my being." By soul, the Hebrews meant the whole being of a person. Blessing the Lord, the parallel construction indicates, means the same as blessing the Lord's name; Hebrews believed that the person was present in his or her name. Sometimes the synonyms do not form a ⚡ cross (chiasm) as in the example above. Another kind of parallel construction is: a _____ b For example:

a _____ b

```
             a                      b
Come! Let us raise a joyful song / to the Lord
             a                      b
  a shout of triumph / to the Rock of our salvation (Ps 95).
```

From the parallelism of the two phrases marked "b", we now know what it means for the Lord to be Lord: it is to be a rock for us, the very steadiness of our salvation.

I would also encourage you, especially in praying the

psalms, to look at various translations, if such are available to you. For example, in the opening verses of Psalm 103 which we have used as an example above, according to the *New English Bible's* translation we read, not "all my being" but "my innermost heart, bless his holy name." A synonym for "soul" in this translation is "innermost heart." Using the variety of translations in your group can increase your appreciation of the rich depth of meaning in Hebrew poetry.

Cursing Psalms

Appreciation of the psalms can be marred, some people think, by the inclusion of cursing psalms in the psalter. Why so much attention to enemies? Throughout Church history these enemies have often been spiritualized into the enemies of the soul, especially vices. Today's liturgists have removed cursing psalms from the Divine Office. Let me make a case for cursing our enemies, always realizing that with God there are no wrong emotions, no negative emotions. We are as he created us—with hatred, jealousy, despair—good. Every emotion is his gift to us, and the cursing psalms can give us a chance to express those emotions in a wholesome way.

I believe there is quite a bit of hypocrisy about violence in our society. William Golding's *Lord of the Flies* has unmasked the vicious child in us who needs to be faced and then befriended. I used to pride myself on my lack of violence and hatred. Why, I'd even turn off the TV in protest over the mildest kind of fistfight. At that time I despised the cursing psalms as primitive, below any Christian to pray. My own hypocrisy or perhaps simple denial of reality came to haunt me when two of our S.S.N.D. sisters came to dinner. They had recently escaped Chile in an outburst of violence by the Pinochet regime. As they told their stories of injustice and atrocity in Chile, my zeal to go to that country burned at fever pitch. After three hours of listening I begged them to stop their stories. Another hour was filled with violent tales. Finally emotion overwhelmed me and I cried, "I would have gone, but I am so angry now that I'd be there only twenty-four hours and I'd have a machine gun in my hands!"

My case for praying cursing psalms comes from my own experience then. First, that violence and hatred of enemies, fury and desire for vindication, are all important aspects of being human. To deny these emotions is to repress a part of our wholesome self and to insure that these same emotions will find a way of asserting themselves, but in covert, twisted ways. God asks us to feel all the parts of our self, to know him as Creator of these emotions, to face them and him together, to let him hear and receive our expression of them in prayer. God knows that we hate and want revenge and are consumed by jealousy. He is himself called a jealous God. Why should we not want with all our heart, as our desiring but frustrated God wants? That is all jealousy is. So we pour out our desires and frustrations, our jealousies, hate, violence to God and we call those outpourings "the cursing psalms." How better to work through these passions but with God?

Secondly, through the 1971 Synod of Bishops, we were alerted to injustice in the world. There are incredible enemies at work against you and me, middle-class members of the first world. Structures of government oppress us. For example, taxes are used to stockpile weapons, cabinet members help despoil our country's resources, congresspeople look the other way as U.S. intelligence agencies plot to interfere in Central America. I need to feel angry, furious at such a government-sponsored fiasco. More than fiasco or mismanagement, it is sin, structural sin. I need God to liberate me and my compatriots from these enemy oppressors. I cry out in prayer and am strengthened to take concrete political action against my enemies. We also have personal enemies who work injustice against us in our neighborhood, our school or shop or firm or hospital or community. We may be physically battered by our husbands, emotionally abused by our wives, or betrayed by our friends. We need to cry out to God with the violence we feel. With him (sometimes with a counselor) we need to admit our feelings, accept our feelings, welcome them as a share in God's own justice, and then give these emotions to the Lord. We can do this through the cursing psalms.

Finally, whenever we pray any of the psalms, formed as community prayer, we pray for the whole Church, our brothers and sisters around the world. Most of the Church lives in the third world, under regimes of crushing oppression, under the despair that is born of hunger. Their enemies are viciously real. When we pray, "May my enemies turn to slime, may all their plans perish," we need to be identified with the poor, to pray out of their hearts. We know how difficult it is to pray when we are sick, even attended by nurses in a gleaming hospital room. Thus we can imagine how difficult it is to pray when one is sick or hungry or frightened in the crowded huts of the poor. We can imagine how hard thousands in concentration camps in Latin America and behind the Iron Curtain might find it to pray and so, for them and with them, we call out curses on their oppressors to a listening God.

Historical Psalms

Another type of psalm that might prove difficult to pray is the historical psalm. We need to understand two experiences of Jewish spirituality to appreciate the use of these psalms in our own lives of prayer. One of the prime tenets of Jewish

spirituality is that remembering makes present. When Israelites of old and Jews today remember the experience of the
exodus, that event is present whether four hundred years later
or three thousand years later. Thus when Jews recount the
wonderful works of God on their behalf, those concrete,
historical situations happen again: God is freeing the oppressed, leading the wandering, raising up armies, defending
the cities, giving the harvest, returning the exiles again. When
they remember God's acts, God acts again, today, for them.

A second point to remember in using these often long
and detailed psalms is that as God has chosen and saved and
cared for a people with a specific, unique history, so he has
chosen and saved and cared for our people in our specific
history. Our people might be the world or nation or neighborhood or family whom God does free and lead and give to
today. "Remember me, Lord, when you save your people,"
the author of Psalm 105 writes. We can use these historical
psalms to recall God's action in our own personal history of
salvation. Like the Israelites, God is leading us personally on a
journey to freedom, on a pilgrimage to himself. Historical
psalms call us to remember his action on our behalf and to
praise and thank him for his constant care (*hesed* and *emet*).
To share the fruits of our remembering with a group reveals to
them our unique salvation history and causes their thanks to
arise with our own. The remembering of even our personal
history invites us to community with others.

Laments, Praise and Thanks

It may be that we were taught never to complain, to hold
back tears, to look for the silver lining, to guard against
depression, especially any loss of heart so deep it might
border on despair. Yet despair is an emotion, part of being

human. The psalmists model these emotions for us as they express their dissatisfaction with the world, themselves, even with God. *"Lamah?"* they cry. "Why?" These psalms take their name, lament, from this Hebrew word. "My tears are my food day and night" (Ps 42). Sometimes the grief is spelled out detail by detail. Nothing is too insignificant to complain about to a God whose unfailing tenderness we trust.

Finally we note that the majority of psalms are full of praise and thanksgiving, with blessings often depicted in great detail. One feature of the psalms is their specific attention to God at work both in the nation and in the feelings of their own hearts. Every action, every thought, every emotion is referred to the Savior God who creates us good. Praise God! Or, in Hebrew, using a short form of Yahweh, "allelu-ya!"

Guided Prayer

Psalm 107:

When in your life have you been lost, hungry and thirsty? When have you been bound in chains or subdued in spirit? When have you been rebellious, repentant and healed? When have you been carried up to heaven and plunged into the depths? When have you been in deserts and when have you found a home? And how have you felt about the Lord during all these times? How do you feel about him as you remember your own salvation history?

Psalm 23:

What are the things which block your response to life, to people, to God? Ask the Lord to reveal these blocks—fears, hostilities, hurts, etc. Then repeat slowly: "I fear no evil for you are with me."

Psalm 23:
When has your response to life, your relationships with people and with God been most satisfying? Ask the Lord to reveal these happy or peaceful times to you. Repeat slowly: "Surely goodness and kindness shall follow me all the days of my life."

Psalm 103:
If your translation reads "praise" change it to "bless," the original Hebrew word. Blessing someone means to exchange life with that person. To bless the Lord is to offer him your life. Note that this psalm deals with sin, and yet we offer a sinful life to him, for he knows that we are dust. Offer him the things about yourself which you really don't like.

Psalm 115:
Here it is the Lord who blesses us, exchanges his life with us—with you. What does it mean for his life to invade you, to permeate you? When have you had such an experience? Ask him to bless you again and again during your day.

Exercises

■ Take five minutes of silence to get in touch with the emotions of the day. Choose a psalm from the catagory that describes your feeling-tone. Take another five minutes to read/pray the psalm. Share your feelings and those parts of the psalm that express you right now.

Praises: 8, 48, 104, 105, 117, 135, 150
Laments: 22, 42, 43, 51, 71, 80
Thanks: 34, 66, 67, 75, 118, 136
Curses: 35, 59, 69, 109, 137, 140

■ Name a favorite psalm and tell why it speaks to you.

■ Rewrite a psalm in your own words. For example, Psalm 23: "The Lord is my leader; I am not afraid to move on."

■ On a very down day, compose your own lament and find someone to pray it with you.

■ For a week pay attention to the news about a certain situation you consider unjust. Get inside the skin of the victims of this injustice and write a prayer, even a cursing prayer, out of their skin. Share these at your next group meeting. You may leave that meeting in tears or furious or discouraged. Give those powerful emotions to the Lord all the way home. Ask him to channel the energy of that emotion into positive action, however small, for justice here or abroad.

For Further Reading

On the psalms:

Dunlop, Laurence. *Patterns of Prayer in the Psalms.* New York: Seabury Press. 1982.
   One of the best books on biblical spirituality I have ever read, although he becomes tedious at the end.

On the situation in Chile, described by our sisters:

Cassidy, Sheila. *Audacity To Believe.* Cleveland: Collins World, 1977.
   Sheila, a medical doctor, was not as fortunate as our sisters to escape. She details her journey with God during long days of imprisonment and torture.

Jesus

6. Jesus

"In the fullness of time, God sent his Son . . ." In this chapter, the centerpiece of this book, about the center of human history, the center of our life, Jesus, I want to change my methodology and begin with exercises, preferably in a group. Then I will comment and offer suggestions for prayer.

Exercises

■ Jesus asked, "Who do people say that I am?" Those words are addressed to us too. Share what people today believe about Jesus. Limit the time of your discussion. Then get personal. "Who do *you* say that I am?" Take five minutes of silent reflection. In a faith sharing style (no discussion, no judgments) tell the group who Jesus is for you personally.

■ Gospels are not historical documents, nor do they offer a biography of Jesus. They are proclamations of the good news about Jesus. Each evangelist and his community remembered different things about Jesus because their memories of him were affected by their own lives. His resurrection, his passion, certain incidents from his life, certain of his words made sense of their own joys and pains, victories and failures. Without copying from any of the four Gospels, or even rereading favorite sections, remember the Gospels and then spend half an hour writing your own gospel. What about all that Jesus did and said is important in your life? That is good news (gospel) for you. Share your gospel with your group. Your family might appreciate hearing it too.

■ Read Luke 24; John 20—21. What similarities between these two accounts of the resurrection can your group find? What differences? Speculate: Why might there be so many differences?

■ Read the passion account in Mark 15. Read John 19. Were there or were there not women at the foot of the cross? Did Jesus cry out, abandoned by God, or was he composed, full of dignity? Discuss. Which portrayal of Jesus speaks more to you? Why? Share that.

■ Listen to "St. Matthew's Passion" by Johann Sebastian Bach. Share your feelings.

■ If God was understood by Jewish authors of Scripture as so passionate, how would you expect to find Jesus, the ultimate expression of God? In your group name all the deeply-felt emotions of Jesus that you can remember. An ancient doctrine of the Church Fathers is: Whatever is not assumed by Christ is not redeemed. This statement, of course, excluded rebellion against God; rebellion is the sin meant by the author of Hebrews when he writes that Jesus is like us in everything but sin (Heb 2:17–18; 4:15). Jesus as completely human would have felt every human passion. Feelings such as lust, greed, jealousy, and hatred are not sinful. They are human and need to be acknowledged so that their power over us can be broken by a liberator God who yearns to set us free. In your group list all kinds of emotions that human beings experience. Using your imaginations and the insights of the Spirit, imagine when Jesus might have fallen in love, when he might have felt greedy, guilty, possessive, confused, etc. Discuss, trying to stay open to even "wild" images. Imagination has power, but remember the Spirit's power to guide the group "in all truth" (Jn 16:13); remember that the Spirit is with you.

■ Gospels have been described as passion accounts with extended introductions. We tend to think of Jesus' suffering as concentrated in his last fifteen to twenty hours. Take five minutes to remember Gospel stories in which Jesus suffered at other times in his life. Share your memories of him.

■ Another way to understand the word "passion" is desire (as, e.g., she has a passion for tennis). What did Jesus passionately desire? What did God passionately desire for Jesus? Some people are afraid to get close to God because, they say, Look what God did to Jesus. They remember, of course, the agony in the garden when Jesus prayed, "Not my will but yours be done" (Mk 14:36). Then the soldiers hauled him off to violence and death. What did God passionately desire for Jesus in the garden? What does God passionately desire for you? Stop and reflect. Sometimes we try to console someone in grief by saying: "This must be God's will." The God I know does not passionately desire anyone's suffering. On the contrary, God passionately *hates* human suffering. No wonder Jesus exhausted himself healing pain and groaned in agony over his friend Lazarus' death. Jesus was mirroring God's desire to heal us. How would you comfort someone in grief? Role-play various responses and come to consensus about the most appropriate.

Through these exercises I hope you have discovered your lively love and admiration for Jesus, but that your beliefs about him vary. Varied understandings of Jesus course through the pages of the New Testament. In other words, we discover many Christologies in the early Church. We can discover many Christologies in today's Church if we honestly speak to each other of who *we* say Christ is.

New Testament Christologies

In the first communities of Christians some thought that Jesus was a prophet, others a wonder-worker. Some thought he would become Messiah (the Christ) at the end of the world, others thought he was made Christ (Messiah) at his resurrection. Mark thinks Jesus became Son of God at his baptism by John; Matthew and Luke believe he was Son of God from the time of his birth; John explains that as Word of God, the uniquely begotten Son of God pre-existed all creation. It took centuries of debate, philosophizing, even war before the Council of Chalcedon in 451 promulgated a "definition" of Jesus Christ. That Council used philosophical categories, language which today confuses rather than clarifies. We stand on surer ground if we describe Jesus rather than try to define him, even try to define (literally, put limits on) the mystery of the incarnation.

The authors of the New Testament did not presume to define; they did not offer a systematic Christology. In John's Gospel, for example, the evangelist contradicts himself about Jesus' relationship with the Father: "The Father and I are one"; "The Father is greater than I." In Paul's letters we find various Christologies as well. What the evangelists did, so beautifully, was tell the story of Jesus in such a way that our own personal stories and the stories of our communities could be engulfed by his, enriched, given meaning. We are meant, through reading the Gospels, to participate in the experiences of Jesus. In John 20:31, the evangelist explains that he has written so that we might have faith that Jesus is the Christ (Messiah; literally the anointed one) and that through faith (knowing him, clinging to him) we may have life.

Therefore, we approach the Gospels to know Jesus, the historical man, to know Christ, the risen Lord always present in his communities. We attend to the truth of his person, not "truths" about him. We don't need to harmonize or unify the four Gospels but we can learn to live with the ambiguities and go beneath the facts of a story to be engaged by the meaning of a story. For example, why does only Luke portray Jesus' crib as a manger, whereas Matthew situates the holy family in a house in Bethlehem? Harmonizers would try to explain the discrepancy by assuring us that after a while there was room in the inn for the newborn and his parents. There is no need to manipulate the Gospels like this. We need to ask Luke's meaning in writing the truth of Jesus' first home. This truth may not correspond to historical fact; the family may indeed have had a house in Bethlehem. Yet for Luke and his community, who understood history differently than we do in an age of instant retrieval of fact, it is important that Jesus' identification with the poor and outcast begins even at birth. Luke symbolizes that identification by having Mary lay Jesus in a manger. That Jesus understands the pain of the poor and wants to share their suffering even from infancy is good news, Gospel for the poor and outcast. Jesus is attractive to them, to us because of this almost insignificant image in Luke's Gospel.

Jesus Reveals Himself Uniquely

If any of the above disturbs you, I strongly recommend the first two small books in the Further Reading section. My purpose in exploring briefly the various Christologies in the

New Testament is to impress on you that faith in Jesus is unique to each of us because Jesus reveals himself to us individually. Of course he reveals himself to communities, as he did to the earliest communities, as he did at the Council of Chalcedon. We, like the bishops and like the grass-roots Christians of the first four centuries, need to discover Jesus in the Gospel of our own lives and to share our discoveries with each other, building community truth. There is such richness if we dare to express who Jesus is in a group. No one's description is wrong because Jesus is the giver of faith; Jesus has revealed himself uniquely to this person in this way.

I have heard parents despair over their teenager's lack of faith. "My son likes Jesus, thinks he's a cool teacher, great pacifist. I try to explain that he is God, and my boy just gives me an exasperated shrug and walks away. If he'd listen I could prove that Jesus is God by using the miracles . . ." So many of us were taught to prove the resurrection, to prove Christ's divinity. Mysteries of faith like the resurrection or Christ's divinity cannot be proved; that which can be proved no longer requires faith.

We, however, became fascinated by our logic, by the reasonableness of a faith that became more and more a deposit of truths which we could hurl at scoffers. Now our own children have become the scoffers. Pope John XXIII understood the exasperated shrugs of a bored world and so called a Council. He urged the bishops to find new interpretations for ancient doctrines, to find new and meaningful language to express our faith.

Incarnation as Process

One of our chief doctrines is the mystery of the incarnation. In pre-Vatican II days we would have been warned away from mysteries as impossible to understand. Why engage in exercises of futility? Now the prominent theologian Karl Rahner writes: mystery is that which is infinitely knowable. A way of approaching the incarnation which has been helpful to me, using today's philosophy and language instead of that of the fifth century, I suggest to you. Certainly we are all more aware of process. Process is as important as product. Growth is a process, not to be hurried. Let us suppose then that the incarnation, the Word of God taking flesh, was a process. Usually we pinpoint the incarnation as a moment of time in Mary's womb. But suppose that the Word of God was ever more and more completely taking flesh, becoming human. We all are in a process of becoming more and more truly human. Why not God's Son? Jesus grew "in wisdom and age and grace," Luke writes.

We and our children are in process of receiving the gift of faith, in process of receiving Jesus' self-revelation. We are at various points in that process. Some of us might quite honestly give intellectual assent to a set of divinely revealed truths; others quite honestly cannot. We will not be saved because of intellectual assent. We will be saved by that faith in Jesus which means relationship with him, knowing him, walking with him, opening to him, trusting him.

This chapter is the centerpiece of our pilgrimage because as we move into the New Testament we want to "keep our eyes fixed on Jesus, on whom faith depends from start to finish" (Heb 12:2). In a more literal translation of the same passage, Jesus is called the "pioneer and perfecter of our faith." Our purpose is to know Jesus. We ask for open hearts so that our "searching the Scriptures" will not be esoteric, merely theoretical. Jesus cries out against the Pharisees:

> You study the Scriptures
> believing that in them you have eternal life;

these Scriptures witness to me,
yet you refuse to come to me for life (Jn 5:39–40).

We study the Scriptures only to come to Jesus for life.
Jewish rabbis taught that to study Scripture is to worship. May
our experience be one of worship as we keep our eyes fixed
on Jesus and study the Scriptures.

Guided Prayer

The Gospels are called "passion accounts with extended
introductions." Of all that we could focus on in the events of
Jesus' life, death and resurrection, we will highlight the passion of Jesus. The following passages carry two meanings of
passion: strong, deep, long-lasting emotion, as well as suffering which permeated Jesus' whole life as it does our own.

Even to read Scripture is to pray. Prayer is a dialogue,
and God speaks to us in his Word. Whatever we think,
whatever we feel, whatever way we respond to the Word is
our part of the dialogue, is prayer.

John 11:38–44:

Jesus stands in pain, in tears before the tomb and calls out for
new life. Lazarus, come forth. He is fully alive. Allow others
to free you of some of your binding forces. In what do you
find joy? Are you glad to be alive? Life, your aliveness is a gift.
With whom is Jesus asking you to share your life now?

Luke 19:41–48; 12:49–52; 13:31–35; Hebrews 5:7;

What do you feel in listening to Jesus express his deep desires,
fears, frustrations, anger? Here is a passionate man. From
where does this intensity come? How do you feel about

human passion, about intense people? Where does *your* passion lie? Talk with Jesus about these aspects of being an alive human being.

Mark 3:20-21; 6:1-5:

Can you identify with Jesus, feel like him, feel rejected (only if at some time in your life you felt rejected)? Can you speak with him about the situation, asking him to talk to you about how he felt? How do you feel toward him as you listen? Speak with him about the incident in your life. How does he feel as he listens to your hurt?

Mark 5:21-24, 35-43:

Identify with Jesus, trying to get deep into his feelings. You are trying to help and everyone laughs at you. Tell your Father how you feel. Ask for what you need. Try to hear-see-sense your Father's response to you.

Matthew 8:19-20:

One of the greatest sufferings these days is constant change and insecurity. Jesus can call no place home; he has no earthly security, has no idea who will care for him in his old age, does not know how long the crowds and the disciples will be with him before they tire of his non-political message. Try to be with Jesus to let him share the insecurities of his life. Then speak with him about your insecurities.

John 6:59-71:

Perhaps one of Jesus' deepest sufferings is expressed in the line: "Will you, also, go away?" What hurts more than the fear of rejection by the very people we thought were friends? He is afraid to be deserted by his friends. He expresses his feelings of fear, anxiety. Can you feel what he is feeling? Have you ever felt left out, left behind? Have you ever felt as though, if your companions ever found out what you were like deep inside, they would walk away from you disgusted? Speak with Jesus about these feelings that you both share.

Contemplation is, simply, looking at Jesus, trying to be with him in his life, trying to feel his feelings. It is a way of letting him share his mind and his heart with us so that when we relate to the body of Christ today we may think his thoughts and love with his love. Some days passages like the last set above may evoke such strong remembrance of our own pain that we have to speak with Jesus about it. Other days we may be drawn to stay with Jesus' feelings rather than our own. Both are excellent ways to pray Scripture.

For Further Reading

Ciuba, Edward. *Who Do You Say That I Am?* New York: Alba House, 1974.
  Father Ciuba carefully but simply explains the Gospels of Matthew, Mark, and Luke using the historical-critical method. His treatment of miracles is helpful as are discussion questions at the end of each chapter. He includes a glossary.

Marrow, Stanley. *The Words of Jesus in Our Gospel: A Catholic Response to Fundamentalism.* New York: Paulist, 1979.
  Father Marrow addresses fundamentalist interpretations of the Gospels. As more and more Christians take the Scriptures literally, Catholics need better helps to interpret Scripture in the face of fundamentalism.

Senior, Donald. *Jesus, A Gospel Portrait*. Dayton: Pflaum, 1975.

Father Senior, in all his books and his tapes, offers a pastoral approach to the Scriptures.

The Gospel According to Luke

7. The Gospel According to Luke

The poet Robert Frost used to say that teachers don't really teach material; rather, a good teacher teaches himself or herself. With twenty-seven books of the New Testament to choose from, I have selected just a few for our focus, but a few that continually nourish and challenge me. I will, in a way, be teaching myself, just as our four evangelists had to select from among many stories and sayings of Jesus and thus teach their unique viewpoint, theology, spirituality.

I have selected Luke's Gospel because of its author's point of view. When one lays this Gospel alongside of Matthew's and Mark's, much of the material is the same. It is, however, Luke's differences from the other two that highlight what was of greatest concern to him and his community. With the rest of the scholarly community, I maintain that Luke the evangelist was neither a companion of Paul, nor a confidant of Mary, nor a physician. Against most of the scholarly community, I believe that he was of the Jewish race but trained by Greeks both in secular subjects and in Scripture. His narrative style is excellent and his biblical spirituality is deep.

84   *Prayer Pilgrimage Through Scripture*

Jesus' Prophetic Spirit and Word

As with each Gospel, Jesus is the centerpiece. Luke envisions Jesus as a prophet, filled with the Spirit to challenge the rich and powerful but particularly to comfort the poor and outcast. The word of God which Jesus preaches is addressed universally to all kinds of people, to all the nations.

Even before Jesus' birth, the Spirit moves powerfully in the lives of Zechariah, Elizabeth and Mary. Their inspired speech and songs are gifts of the Spirit. With the Spirit's power hovering over her, Mary's unique gift of the Spirit is her Son. The same Spirit drives the man Jesus through his ministry. "Jesus, armed with the power of the Spirit, returned to Galilee," came to the synagogue at Nazareth, and, having opened the scroll of Isaiah, proclaimed the beginning of his prophetic service (Lk 4:14–20). The same Spirit will continue Jesus' mission and ministry through the empowering of "the Eleven and the rest of the company" as they wait for the promise of the Father (Lk 24). Indeed, the second volume of Luke's work, Acts of the Apostles, is a kind of Gospel of the Holy Spirit.

The word of God which Jesus wields, like every prophetic word, critiques the rich and powerful of this world. John the Baptizer issues a call for social justice (3:10–16) which Jesus continues. His "woe to you" statements warn the self-satisfied (6:24–26). Simon, his host at a banquet, is unfavorably compared with an infamous woman of the streets (7:36–50). Rich fools, described in 12:13–21, are headed for destruction. Jesus offers a story of such a rich yet stingy man in his parable of Lazarus and Dives (16:19–31) and strikes again at religious "riches" in the parable of the Pharisee and the publican who came to pray (18:10–14).

Through Jesus' prophetic word, God comforts the poor. To be in solidarity with the poor, Jesus would have to know and share their poverty. Luke casts the birth of Jesus in just that way. Far from "home," their roots in Bethlehem, his parents have to journey through territory infested with bandits, find a manger for the child, welcome the poor and outcast shepherds. In the temple his parents make the offering of the poor (2:24). "Blessed are you poor," the adult Jesus addresses the crowds (not like Matthew's "Blessed are the poor in spirit"). These poor are the folks he came to preach good news to:

> The Spirit of the Lord is upon me because he has anointed me; he has sent me to announce good news to the poor, to proclaim release for prisoners and recovery of sight for the blind; to let broken victims go free, to proclaim the year of the Lord's favor" (Lk 4:18–19).

The good news to the poor is that their Father loves them and comes running down the road to meet them, welcome them home, feast them and their friends (the parable of the prodigal son, which might better be titled the story of the prodigal or extravagant father—Lk 15:11–32).

Jesus With Outcasts

Closely linked with the poor in Luke's theology are sinners and outcasts from society. Only Luke carries stories about foreigners who find favor with God, stories in which Jesus praises the widow of Sarepta and Naaman the Syrian (4:25–30). Only Luke hands on two stories of the outcast Samaritans. One is a good and compassionate man who helps victims of violence (10:29–37), and the other is a leper, grateful for Jesus' healing (17:11–19). Tax collectors like Zacchaeus (19:1–10) and thieves crucified with him (23:39–43) are offered reconciliation; both are incidents unique to Luke's Gospel.

Finally, a major class of Jewish outcasts were women. To most husbands, and certainly in the eyes of the teachers of the law, they were property, only a bit more valuable than cattle. Yet in Luke's Gospel they receive a prominent role in Jesus' infancy: Mary, Elizabeth, Anna. To indicate Mary's importance, Luke has Mary receive the angel's message whereas Mary in Matthew's Gospel is kept in the dark while Joseph is told the child's origins and name. When a man is mentioned, a woman is often paired with him: for example, Simeon/Anna; widow of Sarepta/Naaman the Syrian. When a situation appealing to a man is used in Jesus' teaching, the next example often appeals to a woman: shepherd searching for a sheep/woman searching for a coin (15:1–10); the kingdom is like a grain of mustard seed which a man sowed/like leaven which a woman hid in meal (13:18–20). Jonah is a sign/ queen of the south is a sign (11:29–32). Women accompany Jesus as disciples (8: 1–3), entertain him and learn from him as Martha and Mary did (10:38–42). Luke alone hands on the episode of the women weeping as Jesus carries his cross to Calvary (23:27–32).

Three women are carefully depicted with great tenderness by Luke. The first is the prostitute (wrongly identified with Mary Magdalene) who weeps so unabashedly that she washes Jesus' feet with her tears and kisses them. Her great love in action becomes a touchstone for a major message of Jesus in Luke's Gospel: "Her sins are forgiven because she has loved much" (7:36–50). The second woman, like the prostitute, is written about only by Luke. A woman was attending synagogue while Jesus was teaching, a woman bent over for eighteen years; "she could not fully straighten herself." Jesus calls to her and announces her freedom from her handicap. When the president of the synagogue berates, not Jesus, but the people for coming to be healed on the sabbath, Jesus responds harshly that religious leaders wouldn't hesitate to care for their oxen or asses on the sabbath, so why not care for "this woman, a daughter of Abraham?" The woman stands straight and the people rejoice (13:10–17).

The third woman is Mary, the mother of Jesus. The evangelist Mark quickly dismisses Mary after she tries to take Jesus home, sure that he is out of his mind (Mk 3:21. 31). Matthew allows her a role, but quite subordinate to Joseph's in the infancy narratives, his only mention of her. John places her in two key positions: at Cana and at the cross. Luke, however, focuses on her relatives, her activities in the infancy stories and accords her a major hymn, the Magnificat. In a cryptic passage (11:27–28) it seems that Jesus puts down Mary. A woman in the crowd calls out to Jesus: "Blessed is the womb that bore you and the breasts that you sucked." Jesus replies: "Blessed rather are those who hear the word of God and keep it." Luke has set the stage for this little drama in his first chapter when Mary responds, "Be it done to me according to your word" (1:38). Mary is not to be praised for physical motherhood. Jesus again raises women's role in an anti-feminine society, saying in fact that women have every right to be hearers of the word, that is disciples. If anyone "kept" the word of God, it certainly was Mary whom Luke portrays as keeping and pondering the word (2:19, 51). Scripture scholar Raymond Brown calls her the first disciple. Through his narrative Luke calls her a model disciple, one who is taught by God in the depths of her heart.

Forgiveness and Reconciliation

One final unique contribution of Luke to our own spiritual development: instead of Matthew's commission of the risen Lord to teach and baptize, Jesus' disciples in Luke are sent to offer an opportunity for reconciliation, "that repentance and forgiveness of sins should be preached in his name to all nations" (24:47). Luke's entire Gospel could be called good news of reconciliation and forgiveness, a Gospel in which Jesus feels a gut level response of compassion with the sinful, the weak, and the alienated (literally, his bowels are moved with compassion). Jesus images the Father's own compassion. In a dramatic change from Matthew's Gospel, Luke does not ask us to be perfect as our heavenly Father is perfect but, instead, to be compassionate as our heavenly Father is compassionate (6:34–36). When I ask people all over the country to finish the sentence, be you . . . as your heavenly Father is . . . a unanimous chorus of "perfect" resounds. Perhaps only five percent have ever even heard of Luke's version, "Be you compassionate as your heavenly Father is compassionate." Yet the people I meet in class or in spiritual direction tell me their goal in life is "to love well." How encouraging, then, is Luke's message to love well, to grow in compassion. Jesus of Luke's gospel not only urges us but models so well a Spirit-filled life of attention to and care for God's poor and those crushed in spirit. Jesus commissions us too to offer compassion, forgiveness, and reconciliation to all the peoples.

Luke's Gospel currently is receiving attention from scholars and laity alike. As the Church community becomes more imbued with a call and commitment to social justice, Jesus in Luke's Gospel offers a model for attending to the needs of the poor and the outcast. A renewal of the Spirit's outpouring is the felt experience of many Christians in our day. "Jesus, driven by the power of the Spirit" (Lk 4:14), comes in our time to preach a word of comfort to the downtrodden, a word of challenge to the comfortable through our own prophetic mission and ministry as Church. The Spirit impels us, as disciples of Jesus, to a universal compassion, to a global reconciliation. We are comforted and challenged ourselves in those tasks as we read and pray with Luke's Gospel.

Guided Prayer

Read Luke 1:26-38:
Where did the message from the Lord come to Mary? Was she cooking, working in the fields, drawing water? Where does the Lord's message come to you? She is confused and fearful. What messages of the Lord have confused and frightened you? Talk them over with him. "The Holy Spirit will overshadow you." In Genesis the Spirit overshadows the waters of chaos and brings life from whatever seems empty. Ask the Spirit to bring life and peace to whatever seems void, chaotic in your life.

Luke 7:36-50:
Our relationship to Jesus often swings between centering on our needs and looking to him. This woman asks for nothing; she simply expresses her admiration and love. Try looking at her with admiration and love, then at Jesus.

Luke 4:1-13:
Identify with Jesus being led by the Spirit into the desert. Feel the hot wind, the sand, the hunger. Tell the Holy Spirit how you feel interiorly.

Luke 22:42-44:
Look at Jesus, feel with Jesus in this experience of anxiety before his suffering. In looking at him, try to use as many of your senses as you can—can you hear the trees in the garden rustling, can you feel the wind, can you smell the fresh

crispness of the night? In feeling with him, let your own anxieties surface. What worries you, of what are you afraid, what do you dread? Let your stomach knot up, your head throb if need be. Share your emotions with Jesus. Then try to listen as he talks about his fears and try to comfort him, understand him (which is a comfort). Remember that contemplation is, simply, looking at Jesus, trying to be with him in his life, trying to feel his feelings. It is a way of letting him share his mind and his heart with us so that when we relate to the body of Christ, the Church-community of today, we may think his thoughts and love with his love.

Luke 24:33–53:

The disciples who met Jesus on the road to Emmaus returned to find that "the Eleven and the rest of the company had assembled." Mary was probably one of that "company." Put yourself in Mary's place and let the events of verses 33–53 happen to you—as Mary. Tell Jesus how you feel. You, as Mary, are commissioned to bring forgiveness to people. Has Mary interceded for you, to bring you God's forgiveness? How and for whom will you intercede—in prayer, in action, by your words, your acceptance, your offering of comfort?

Exercises

■ Remember that a Gospel is good news about Jesus Christ. It is not history, it is not biography. If you were an evangelist how would you write the story of Jesus in order to attract others to him? What good news about him would you focus on? It has been at least a week since you wrote a gospel as an activity in the Jesus chapter. You are different now. You were influenced by Gospels written by others. Take five minutes to remember the stories and Gospel experiences that you can remember. Which ones speak good news to you— personally? No checking the text. Remembering is the key. For the next fifteen minutes, write a brief gospel. As you put down your pen at the end, pay attention to how you feel. Share your gospel out loud; then share your feelings. In order to keep within time limits you may have to subdivide your group. Later, alone, compare your two gospels. What are the similarities, what are the differences? What do they mean?

■ Plan to serve coffee and cake to your group tonight. Leave two chairs empty. Read Luke 14:12–14. Then invite Jesus to come to your table and to bring one of his friends. Go around the group and let each one name Jesus' friend, some- one or some type of person we despise or disdain. For example, I might say, "Jesus is bringing Fernando Marcos with him here tonight." Leave silent time for the group to image Jesus and the dictator of the Philippines seating them- selves with the group. Let the group pray silently as well. Someone might suggest a type of person such as homosexuals or ex-convicts or white-collar criminals. After the experience, ask the group how each felt. There may be anger expressed, or indignation: "Surely Jesus wouldn't bring such and such a character with him!" Don't argue or defend, just listen and receive. St. Paul warns us that Jesus is a scandal.

■ I briefly treat two stories, that of the prostitute washing Jesus' feet and that of the woman bent for eighteen years. Your group can explore so much more deeply God's revela- tion of his compassion from these incidents. Read Luke 7:36– 50 aloud. Then reread it. This time pause every few verses and let anyone share an insight or feeling that the lines trigger. Don't worry about silences. Use the same technique on Luke

13:10–17, although you may want to save it for another meeting. This is not really discussion, let alone argument. You can build on each other's comments but not contradict.

For Further Reading

Cardenal, Ernesto. *The Gospel in Solentiname* (4 vols). Mary-
    knoll, N.Y.: Orbis Books, 1976.
*This book uses the technique of Gospel sharing that I
propose in the last exercise. These peasants and fisherfolk of
Nicaragua comment verse by verse on Gospel passages with
a profound wisdom derived from their lived experience of
God in the midst of their poverty.*

Karris, Robert. *Invitation to Luke*. Garden City, N.Y.: Double-
    day, 1977.
    What Are They Saying About Luke and Acts? New
York: Paulist, 1979.
*Father Karris writes a commentary that is easy to fol-
low; his contribution to the Paulist series* What Are They
Saying About . . . *is valuable.*

Johnson, Luke. *Sharing Possessions: Mandate and Symbol of
    Faith.* Philadelphia: Fortress Press, 1981.
*The scholarship is evident but the spiritual dimension is
equally profound. This is the type of book useful for medita-
tion; it is possibly a life-changing book.*

The Gospel
According to John

8. The Gospel According to John

In this Gospel once again we learn that God takes the initiative, inviting us to union with him and with each other. "In the beginning was the Word." From the beginning God has tried to communicate his love, his blessing, his very self to us. "In various and fragmented ways, God spoke through the prophets . . . but in these days he has spoken through his Son" (Heb 1:1–2). In times past God tried to show his care through the law "given through Moses, but now grace and truth have come through Jesus Christ" (Jn 1:16–17). Grace and truth are the translations of *hesed* and *emet*. God who showered, even overwhelmed his people with *hesed* and *emet* throughout their stormy history offers the final, total gift of himself. Jesus embodies, lives out in his body, God's *hesed* and *emet*. God's inner life is spelled out for us by the outward life of Jesus. "No one has ever seen God, but the Son, who is closest to the Father's heart, he has made God known" (Jn 1:18). The center of John's writing then is God, but God made visible in the human life of Jesus, God communicated to us by the abiding life of the Spirit, the Paraclete. We will first focus on Jesus as John and his community understood him; then we will reflect on the work of the Paraclete.

Over the decades, from the time the Beloved Disciple,

often called John the evangelist, knew Jesus in the flesh until members of John's community put the finishing touches on the Fourth Gospel and John's First Epistle, many ideas about Jesus, many Christologies, were current in the various Christian communities. Like Luke, John understood Jesus as a prophet, but one greater than Moses; Jesus was portrayed as king, as shepherd, as vine. Of all the Christologies found in John's Gospel, for purposes of space we will only attend to Jesus as revealer of the Father and as agent of the Father.

Jesus, The Embodiment of God

If we want to know what God is like, the Johannine community insists, we need only look at the historical life of Jesus. The Word of God made flesh is the perfect expression of God. This is, of course, the meaning of the word incarnation; its Latin root *carne* means flesh. John portrays Jesus as divine more than any other evangelist, yet portrays him as more deeply human, more "fleshy," than the others. Jesus is capable of that deep and sustained emotion which so characterizes our humanity. Three incidents will illustrate the point. We can see his fear, his frustrated fury and his tenderness.

Jesus has delivered a "hard saying" about eating and drinking his body and blood. Even his disciples walk away from him muttering. That most painful of human emotions, one that erodes our basic trust, wells up in Jesus. He is afraid to be abandoned. Then he turns to the Twelve: "Will you also go away?" (Jn 6:59–71). How often has God not questioned his fickle people, Israel, about their loyalties, and now Jesus asks the question in a simple, unmistakable way. God's fidelity, *emet*, will last forever regardless of our walking away. Jesus embodies God's fidelity here, feeling in his human heart the pain of possible desertion.

God hates all that oppresses. Indeed, the Jewish Scriptures constantly record God's combat against forces of evil, alienation, injustice. Jesus puts flesh on this yearning of God to smash evil once for all. Death is the symbol and experience of ultimate evil. Jesus goes to Lazarus' tomb and there both groans in hatred of death and weeps in compassion with Mary of Bethany (Jn 11:38–44). God's own *hesed* and *emet* are embodied there at the grave.

God's extravagant love, *hesed*, has always been at the service of his people. Perhaps no other Gospel story so dramatically shows Jesus imaging God's own tenderness to us as the footwashing scene at the Last Supper. Perhaps no other experience for the majority of us so captures our tragic flaw: like Peter, we refuse to be served. We will be in control, whether over our dirty feet or our complex lives. In his Pulitzer-prize winning book, *Denial of Death*, Ernst Becker lays bare our refusal to be creature. The incident between Jesus and Peter exposed this root sin long ago. Peter will not receive the love and service of God, incarnated in the service, the tenderness of Jesus' action. To refuse to receive is to deny who we are and our dependence on God's care.

Why is it important for us to take the incarnation so seriously? Because Jesus teaches us to reverence our own *carne*, our flesh, to appreciate God's action in and through our bodies, our emotions. God continues to take flesh in us, who are the body of Christ today. We are the ones called to embody God's *hesed* and *emet* today. We do that not only through our minds and wills but through our bodies in all their glory and with all their limitations. Biblical spirituality and incarnational spirituality are two sides of the same coin.

Finally, we might also call Jesus the sacrament of God, a sign of God's presence and activity in the world. A sacrament "is an outward sign . . . which gives grace." Jesus is a sign of God who gives grace. He comes that we might have life,

God's own life, and have it in abundance (Jn 10:10). Jesus is translucent. To look at Jesus is to see through him to see God. In John's Gospel there is no scene of transfiguration on Mount Tabor. Instead, the whole of Jesus' life and death is full of light and glory, the very light and glory of God.

Jesus, Agent of the Father

In John's Gospel Jesus is portrayed as agent of the Father. The expression and embodiment of God, Jesus represents God in the flesh. John characterizes Jesus as both disciple and apostle. Some Jewish background is important here. In a missionary thrust throughout the cities of the empire, the prominent rabbis in Israel trained disciples to carry their message. Disciples not only were to memorize the words of their teacher but were to imitate the rabbi in everything: dress, walk, table manners, laugh. Thus when a disciple arrived in a distant spot, the rabbi himself was present through his agent.

Jesus, in John's Gospel, is the disciple of his Father. He does nothing on his own, but only what he sees his Father doing (5:19). He speaks nothing but what he hears from his Father (14:24). He does only the works of his Father (5:17). He reveals all the Father has revealed to him (15:15). As disciple (from the Latin *discipulus*, which means learner) Jesus has learned from God and, more then merely imitating God, embodies God's work in the world.

An agent not only learns from the master teacher but then is sent on mission. Throughout the Fourth Gospel Jesus refers to his being sent from God. He is sent to bring life, "life in abundance" (10:10), to teach the truth that sets us free (8:31–32), to offer the love the Father has offered him (15:9), to create friendship by sharing everything he knows and is, everything he has received from his Father (8:42). Jesus is sent to bring acceptance (the Samaritan woman, Chapter 4), healing (the man born blind, Chapter 9), forgiveness (20:23), the good news that we are loved (3:16). As missioned by the Father Jesus offers peace "not as the world gives" (14:27) and joy, "that your joy may be full" (16:24). Without a doubt, however, Jesus' greatest gift is the Spirit.

The Paraclete

The fourth evangelist calls the Spirit the Paraclete, sometimes translated the comforter, the counselor, the advocate. From its Greek roots, however, Paraclete means one who calls another forward. The priest-poet Gerard Manley Hopkins in a sermon used the image of the Paraclete as a sports' coach, urging us on as we round the bases, calling: "Come on, come on, you can do it!"

In the Last Supper discourse, that long and intimate conversation of Jesus and his friends, Jesus is concerned that we not be left orphans after his death. He describes how the Paraclete will act in his stead and on our behalf. As an abiding, comforting presence, the Spirit will live in us (14:17). From within us, he will teach us everything and call to our minds Jesus' own teaching (14:26). Jesus calls the Paraclete the Spirit of truth who will witness to Jesus, just as his friends will find courage to witness (15:26–27). As Spirit of truth, he will convict the world of its evil, and will be the way we can discern good and evil (16:8–11). As Jesus learned from the Father, so the Spirit "will not speak on his own authority, but will tell only what he hears. He will reveal things that are to come." In fact, Jesus promises that the Spirit will guide us into all truth (16:13). The Spirit will draw everything from Jesus in order to teach us, and in that way he will glorify Jesus (16:14).

After such emphasis on the Spirit of truth in the Fourth Gospel's long and profound discourse, we may lose sight of Jesus' more intimate promise of the Spirit. In the temple, Jesus cries out with eager longing:

> If anyone is thirsty, let that one come to me. Whoever believes in me, let that one drink. As Scripture says, "Streams of living water will flow out from within." Jesus was speaking of the Spirit who believers in him would receive later; for the Spirit had not yet been given because Jesus had not yet been glorified (Jn 7:38–39).

The Spirit is like a fountain of living water, welling up from within us, soothing, healing, satisfying our various thirsts. The gentle and intimate flow of the Spirit, promised here, is fulfilled on Easter night. Jesus breathes on his disciples, inviting them to receive the Holy Spirit who will be the ultimate instrument of peace and forgiveness of sin (20:21–23).

In John's Gospel the Father, Son and Paraclete are central. God initiates dialogue, relationship. We respond to the outpouring of his unconditional love and fidelity, this "grace upon grace" received from the fullness of Jesus himself (Jn 1:16). The fourth evangelist offers us a way to respond. "This is the work that God wants: believe in the one he has sent" (Jn 6:29). The evangelist writes his Gospel that we might believe (Jn 20:31). John's purpose blends with Jesus' purpose; Jesus in John's Gospel prays that we might be one, dies that we might be one, united with him and with each other. Let us first attend to John's purpose—to lead us to believe—and then to Jesus' purpose—to effect unity among believers.

Faith and Unity

Believing for the Jews was not intellectual assent to divinely revealed truths. It was not ascribing to untainted doctrine or absolute truth. Believing for John and his community was wholehearted attachment to God and to Jesus, a basic trust in God's fidelity. Believing was not a habit or virtue of the mind so much as it was a habit of will and affection. To respond to God's initiating love made tangible in his Son Jesus was to be attracted to Jesus, to know him, to be his disciples, to be sent with him as apostles. To believe in Jesus was to cling to him, to be intimately united with him, to share mind and heart with him, to be committed to him. To believe is to accept Jesus' claim on our mind, our wills, our emotions, our bodies, our whole lives.

In this Gospel we notice how Jesus attracts people, literally draws them to himself. If Jesus is lifted up, John repeatedly tells us that he will draw all people to himself. To attract means, from its Latin origins, to draw. Throughout this Gospel, Jesus draws people. In the Gospel's opening scene at the Jordan River, Jesus invites John the Baptist's disciples to "come and see" where he lives (1:38). Andrew brings Peter and Philip brings Nathaniel to this attractive new rabbi. The Pharisee Nicodemus risks his status to speak with Jesus by night; sparked by that dialogue (3:1–15), Nicodemus' courage grows (7:51) until finally his attraction to Jesus is so complete that he boldly asks Pilate for Jesus' dead body (19:39–41). The Samaritan woman is drawn to him (Jn 4) as is Martha (Jn 11), for the evangelist makes it obvious that Jesus respects women's ability to discuss and comprehend theology. The Twelve are attached to him although others walk away (6:66–68); the Beloved Disciple's attraction pulls him even to Calvary. Only in John's Gospel is Mary, his mother, drawn to the cross. Only in John's Gospel do we find Jesus' two dear friends clinging (Mary Magdalene—20:10–18) and jumping overboard (Peter—21:4–8) to express their joy at his resurrection.

In times of crisis too, Jesus attracts: at Cana (2:1–11), in the storm at sea (6:16–21), feeding the hungry with loaves and fish (6:1–13). No one who comes to him will be cast out (6:37). Instead, "the whole world has gone after him" (12:19). When even the Greeks are attracted to him (12:20–21), Jesus knows that his hour has come. The arrival of these non-Jews signals that in "his hour," in being lifted up on the cross, Jesus literally has drawn all people to himself. All these Gospel characters are drawn to Jesus that they might receive the life in abundance which he was sent to bring. Life, life that will last forever, is this, Jesus explains at the Last Supper: to know the one true God and the one whom God has sent (17:3). To come to Jesus is to know God, not only by the workings of our minds, but, as the Jews used the word, by the clinging of our hearts. To know is to be intimately united with. Like the Gospel characters, we can be drawn to "the way, the truth and the life" who is Jesus (14:6). He promises that if we make his word our home, we will be his disciples—that is, we will learn from him, we will know the truth, and the truth will set us free (8:31–32).

Then, like the Gospel characters, we who have been drawn to him will be sent away. Notice how Andrew rushes off to bring Peter, Philip to find Nathaniel, the Samaritan woman to her townspeople, Martha to her sister Mary, Mary Magdalene to tell the brothers that Jesus has risen. To be a disciple, to know truth, to be set free impels us to share that good news with others. To be a disciple will necessarily lead to being an apostle, one sent. All of this—being attracted, knowing, being sent—spells out what John means when he writes this Gospel so that we may believe and, through believing, have life (20:31).

John depicts Jesus, hungry for what God wants (4:34), with his own desires on the night before he dies: "That they all may be one as we are one . . . Father, as you are in me and I am in you, that they may be one in us" (17:12. 21). Mark, Matthew, Luke and Paul note other meanings for the death of Jesus, but John and his community spell out their understanding in terms of unity. Jesus died "to gather into one family all the scattered children of God" (11:52). When he is lifted up on the cross, Jesus draws every believer to himself, uniting us all in his centrifugal force. Just as he united, while hanging on the cross, Mary his mother with the Beloved Disciple, so he unites believers through the centuries, creating us as new family, his family, that we may be one in him.

Guided Prayer

"This is eternal life—to know you, the one true (faithful) God and the one whom he has sent" (Jn 17:3):
To the Jews, to study Scripture *is* to worship. Have you ever experienced union with God even as you listened to or read or studied his word or theology? Let your memory stay with that experience. What feelings arise in you? Share those feelings with the Lord.

"I will give you fountains of living water" (Jn 7:38):
What blocks you from living life in its abundance? Is there a boulder blocking that fountain within you, blocking the spring of living water? Speak with Jesus about your blocks. Where is the "water" stagnant in your life? What do you want from the Lord?

John 6:66-71:

Jesus is afraid to be deserted by his friends. He expresses his feelings of fear, anxiety. Identify with Jesus, surrounded by his friends. How do *you* feel? Tell your Father.

John 11:20-40:

Martha is an initiator. She has an adult relationship with Jesus. How does Martha relate to your personality? How does Jesus feel about her? How does he feel about the Martha in you and/or in those around you?

John 11:45-53:

Jesus died to gather all the scattered children of God. In what ways are you scattered? pulled apart? not whole? not integrated? Ask Jesus to gather you. Where in your families, communities, world interests do you need the power of Jesus' death to gather people together? Pray for these situations.

Focus on Jesus and ask him if it is worth his dying. Ask him why gathering his people was so important to him. Keep a mental image of Jesus on the cross with the peoples of all nations and times—and yourself—coming to him. Ask him how he feels; respond to his feelings.

John 13:1-15; return to verses 3-7:

Peter refuses to be served. He cannot believe that Jesus could love him that much. Jesus wants to kneel before you; he wants to serve you. How do you feel about that desire of his? Talk with him about it.

John 14:22-26:

Friends teach one another. Who are the best teachers you ever had? What made them good teachers? What in you made you able to learn from them? What did they touch in you? What did you open to them? Jesus has called you to learn of him, *to know him*. What are you most glad he has taught you? What do you want him to teach/touch in you now: senses? heart? feelings? desires? intellect? memory? Talk to him as your teacher/friend.

John 15:14–17; 14:15–17:
You are the one whom Jesus calls "friend." His whole life expresses his consuming desire to be with you. Now he promises you his own Spirit, not just to be with you but to live (be alive, moving) within you. Hear his promise ring within you. How do you feel about his desire to share your life? Tell Jesus what it means to you to have him be so intimately present to you. What do you want to share with him? You are sent, too, to share your life and spirit with one another, five others, fifty others. To whom are you sent? How do you feel about being sent? Talk with Jesus about these feelings.

John 16:12–15:
In this passage you are promised truth. Why? The truth will set you free. What is your deepest experience of freedom? Do you sense yourself being truly *your* self in that freedom? Relish that freedom now with Jesus and his Spirit. How were you brought to that freedom? Who was the human instrument or what was the historical event that helped you to freedom? What about now? Is there something in your life nagging you, binding you? How Jesus wants to free you! How his Spirit wants to guide you into freeing truth! Show him what traps you. Plead with Jesus' Spirit (your Advocate) to glorify Jesus in you by setting you free.

You are sent, too, to help others become more free, to be the instrument of Jesus' freeing action. To whom are you sent? How do you feel about being sent? Talk with Jesus about what you can do to create more of an atmosphere of freedom in your community, among your friends, among your co-workers.

John 15:1-12:

Jesus deeply, passionately desires that you be in union with him. He is sent to effect that union. Remember the times you felt united with him and/or with others as branches on a vine. In some manuscripts, verse 11 reads: ". . . so that my joy may be in you, and your joy complete," and other manuscripts read: ". . . so that I may have joy in you and your joy may be complete." Can you believe that second reading? Can you hear Jesus speak directly to you, tell you that you are the cause of his emotion? How do you feel? Speak with him about these feelings. Like him, the vine, you are sent to help others live life, life in abundance. How can you pass on the life you receive from the true vine, Jesus? To whom will you pass on life in abundance today?

John 17:

You are in the Last Supper room, seeing, hearing, smelling, perhaps tasting the remains of the meal. Jesus begins to pray. Now read (perhaps out loud) Jesus' prayer in Chapter 17. When you have finished, go over to where Jesus is sitting. What do you want to tell him? What effect would his praying for them have on the disciples, on their unity? Whom among your family and friends would you want Jesus to pray for, to unite?

John 21:1-13:

Imagine the scene; smell the water, the fish, etc. Are you able to identify better with Peter or with the one whom Jesus loved? Do you recognize Jesus in your life? Do you "jump in" at once just to be with him—or are you hesitating to get close to him? He wants to feed you, to serve you. How do you feel about that? Tell him.

Exercises

■ We find rich and earthy symbols in John's Gospel. Read the Cana story aloud (2:1–11). Then in silence ask each member of your group to sip a glass of water. Next, ask them to sip a glass of wine (have some grape juice on hand should someone prefer it). After about 10–15 minutes of silent tasting, share what these symbols said to you.

■ Another time, the group might spend ten minutes of silent contemplation of a candle (or, if possible, a fire in a fireplace) and share feelings and insights on Jesus as light. A vine or even a philodendron plant could lead to contemplation of Jesus as the true vine and ourselves as branches.

■ Wash one another's feet. Share feelings about it afterward. Why is it so difficult for so many of us to receive service, care, affection? What do you want to do about your hesitations and fears?

For Further Reading

Brown, Raymond E. *The Community of the Beloved Disciple*. New York: Paulist Press, 1979.
A bit technical but sure to be a classic.

MacRae, George. *Invitation to John*. Garden City, N.Y.: Doubleday, 1978.
This series is quite readable. Father MacRae is a giant in Johannine studies.

Newbigin, Lesslie. *The Light Has Come*. Grand Rapids: Wm. B. Eerdmans Publishing Co., 1982.

   A book which can lead to prayer. The author of this exposition is a missionary bishop who is obviously a reflective, prayerful man.

Paul's Letter
to the Galatians

9. Paul's Letter to the Galatians

This letter, one of Paul's earliest, is also one of his most autobiographical. In it, while coping with urgent problems presented by the young Christians from Galatia, Paul presents himself as one who is chosen, missioned and free.

God has taken the initiative in Paul's life—but only after Paul had struggled for control, not only of his life but also of his salvation. Paul worked to save himself by means of the law. Then, one day on the road to Damascus, this zealous Pharisee met the risen Lord who turned his heart and mind around. A change of mind, or *metanoia* in Greek, is often translated "conversion" in English. Paul's conversion however was not from a life of wickedness, nor from Judaism to Christianity. Paul was converted from his attitude of self-righteousness. He was set free from needing to prove himself to God. God already loved him, and had chosen him from his mother's womb.

Chosen, Missioned and Free

Because in his conversion experience he learned that to persecute Christians is to persecute Christ (Acts 9:4), Paul found himself in solidarity with others whether Jew or Gentile, slave or free, male or female (Gal 3:28). He was missioned to them, particularly to the Gentiles, although we find that he also esteemed slaves and women because they were "in Christ." To be missioned is to be sent, *apostello* in Greek, from which comes our word "apostle." Paul considered himself to be an apostle. He spends the first two chapters of this letter defending his identity as an apostle. Many of us think that there are only twelve apostles, yet Barnabas and Paul are called apostles (Acts 14:14). For Luke, the author of Acts, an apostle is a male who has walked with Jesus from the time of his baptism in the Jordan (Acts 1:21–22). There are only twelve because that number is symbolic for Luke of the twelve tribes of God's new chosen people, a new Israel who is the Christian community.

Paul's criteria for what constitutes an apostle differs. An apostle, according to Paul, is one who has experienced that Christ is risen, alive, and present and who is missioned by Christ (1 Cor 15). We cannot qualify for apostleship according to Luke's criteria, but, according to Paul's, every Christian is chosen to be an apostle. In fact, to be baptized is to be an apostle. Once we believed that the lay apostolate was our participation in the work of the bishops who were the true successors to the apostles. We had a mission and ministry in the Church only because the bishops (and, by extension, the priests) invited us to share their ministry. In these days we have discovered what baptism actually means, how baptism creates us as sharers in Christ's own mission and ministry, that the laity have a mission and ministry because we all are the Church.

Chosen and missioned by God, Paul receives a new freedom. Although it may be almost twenty years since his conversion, in his Letter to the Galatians Paul asserts again and again a core experience for him: that Christ has set us free from the law (Gal 5:1). Salvation is God's gift freely given, not a reward for our good behavior. When Paul preached this good news of freedom, the Galatians had accepted the Gospel. After Paul moved on, however, some Judaizers, Christians who were Jewish by race, but who had come to believe that Jesus was the promised Messiah, arrived in the Galatian community. They, who were to trouble Paul during most of his apostolic life, insisted that Gentile Christians be circumcised and keep the Jewish law. Judaizing Christians taught Gentile converts that they first had to become Jews. Paul's anger in this letter is directed both at these Judaizing Christian missionaries and at the Galatians who trusted their law-centered rather than Christ-centered teaching.

Adult Morality

In insisting that Christians are free from the law of the Jews, Paul is hardly preaching immoral or amoral behavior. He realizes that children need rules and regulations to build habits of discipline (Gal 3:24–25). That kind of morality, a kind of taboo mentality which fears and avoids punishment, may be normal for children but not for us who are mature Christians. Christ, according to the theme that runs through this letter, has set us free from the law and all the taboos and guilt associated with it. In other words, our faith in Christ leads us to an adult morality. Faith means our attachment to Christ, our welcome of his claim on our entire lives. This adult morality springs from faith which is characterized by our loving response to God's first having loved us. God initiates our morality, our salvation by his love and fidelity. Our response of love and fidelity is free and freeing, truly an adult morality.

In this Letter Paul gives indications of how he has responded in adult fashion to God's choice of him. He is obedient, concerned for the poor, prayerful and united with Christ. He is not afraid to submit his ideas to dialogue with authority (Gal 2:2, 9). Being in union with the other apostles is more important to him than any righteous proclamation of truth as he sees it. Paul has been converted from self-righteousness and has learned a new kind of obedience, not a slavish, fearful adherence to law and regulations, but an obedience based on dialogue in which he remains flexible and free. The apostles James, John and Cephas (Peter), offering him fellowship, ask him in his mission to the Gentiles to remember the poor which, indeed, Paul was eager to do (Gal 2:9–10).

As for ourselves, being freed from the law does not lead us to lawlessness but to a creative fidelity, to dialogue, to obedience. Being freed from the law, its demands, scrupulous self-centering, allows our energies to be devoted to service and care for the poor. Being freed from the law reminds us that Jesus, not our own works and merits, saves.

Paul makes a profound statement in this early Letter which becomes a cornerstone of his theology. He is keenly aware that the Spirit lives and moves in his heart, crying "Abba! Father!" (Gal 4:6). That same Spirit, keeping him prayerfully united with God, is the source of his astounding experience: "It is no longer I who live, but Christ lives in me" (Gal 2:20). This is the key to an adult morality: the Spirit moves us interiorly, transforming our lives gradually into an expression of Christ's own life present and operating today. In Matthew's Gospel we are enjoined to see and to care for Christ in the least of our brothers and sisters (Mt 25). Some Christians can see Christ in others, others cannot. Another way of responding to the risen Christ still present among us is

Paul's: Christ is at work, caring and healing and freeing and teaching and doing justice for the outcasts in and through us. Instead of seeing Christ in others, we are united with Christ within us. This Pauline experience grounds the teaching of Pope Pius XII in his encyclical on the body of Christ. In 1943 the Pope wrote that we the Church, the body of Christ, *are* Jesus Christ extended in space and time and communicated to humankind. The risen Lord is present and active through the presence and activity of every baptized Christian. We make Jesus present to today's world, to our country, our neighborhood, community, family. We may be free from the law, but to offer our life in faith, to invite the Spirit to transform us into Christ, calls for a mature response, an adult morality. It calls for freedom. "For freedom, Christ has set you free. Let no one make you a slave again" (Gal 5:1).

Guided Prayer

Read Galatians 1 and 2:
The Lord set Paul apart from birth to proclaim the Gospel to the Gentiles. Reflect on the Lord's choosing you as his own "from your mother's womb." When, where, how has his choosing you continued throughout your life? Ask him to show you his presence throughout your life. Listen to him answer you. Tell him how you feel about this choice and this presence.

Read Galatians 1 and 2
What gifts has the Lord given you? Ask him—don't try to think and introspect; let it "come" to you as you try to listen to his answer. What is his purpose in gifting you? Ask him. Listen. Tell him how you feel about his gifts to you.

Read Galatians 2:20—3:6:

Paul asks how the Galatians came to receive the Spirit—through keeping the law or believing the Gospel message? How have you come to receive the Spirit? Why does the Father love you—because you keep the Commandments or because you love and follow Jesus? Ask him what makes you so pleasing to him.

Galatians 3:19-25:

In the Father's plan, we as youngsters learned and practiced the Jewish law. It was like a tutor, but Jesus has called us to make adult decisions, to learn from him day by day how to cling to him (for that is what Paul means by "faith": clinging to Jesus). What is more satisfying to you—a set code which you thought established your security with God or a growing relationship with God's Son which gives you another kind of security? Be honest as you discuss this with him. The law *does* make us secure and we may have to beg him to help us find all our security in him, not even in his law.

Galatians 3:28:

"In Christ there is neither Jew nor Gentile, neither slave nor free person, neither male nor female." Can you remember a time when you felt discriminated against? Was it because you were a woman or a Catholic or of a certain nationality or economic class? Remember the incident as vividly as possible; see the people involved; hear them; refeel your emotions at the time. Then stop. Watch Jesus walk into the situation. What does he do, say? To you, to the other(s)? How can you respond to him? Pray to have racism, classism, sexism, nationalism removed from you and from the Church around the world.

Galatians 4:31—5:6:

Mortal sin means that we choose to cut ourselves off completely from Christ. What does Paul call "mortal sin" in this section? How do you feel about it? Discuss it with Jesus. Ask *him* if Paul is off the wall, if that's how you feel about it. Remember that freedom is frightening, risky and calls for response-ability. The freedom offered us by Jesus calls for an hour-by-hour response to him and to the needs of his people.

Galatians 5:1:

"For freedom Christ has set you free. Let no one make you a slave again." In the past, who or what has enslaved you? How were you set free? How does the memory make you feel? Tell the Lord about your memories and feelings. Ask *him* (not yourself) where he still wants to free you.

Galatians 5:13—6:2:

What is the law of Christ? How do we fulfill it? (See verses 18 and 25.) Ask for the fullness of the Spirit who is love and burden-bearer. He is your power to love. Share some of your burdens in loving with him.

Galatians 5:22:

Use Galatians 5:22 as a criterion to judge your actions and to make your decisions. Do the decisions you make help you to grow in peace, joy, love, kindness, etc.? Remember a major decision you made this past year. Ask the Lord to show you how the fruits of the Spirit have deepened through this decision.

Galatians 5:13—6:2:

After some activity today, stop, read Galatians 5:22. What fruits of the Spirit were present in that activity? How do you feel about that? After some decision you make today, stop, and then read 5:22. What fruits did you experience after making that decision? How will you respond to the Spirit?

Exercises

■ Brainstorm together (no discussion is allowed in brainstorming) a list of taboos, be they religious, cultural (like table manners), or family (like putting the toilet seat down). Then reflect in silence: What taboos have you outgrown? What taboos has Jesus freed you from? After reflection time, share with your group those new freedoms you have experienced (you do not have to bare your whole life; choose those which are appropriate to the level of trust in your group). After the sharing, get in touch with how you feel as you listen to stories of freedom; share your feelings with your group.

■ What does Paul mean when he writes, "You who would be justified (saved) by the law, you are completely cut off from Christ, you have fallen away from grace" (Gal 5:4)? In the Acts of the Apostles (15:9–11), Peter says to the young congregation that keeping the law is an impossible burden, and since the new Christians were saved by grace, not by the law, why impose the law on Gentile converts? Salvation, according to Ephesians 2:4–10, is not a reward for any work we do but God's free gift. Have you ever tried to win God's approval by doing good works? Can you believe that you already have God's approval, that his love for you is unconditional, extravagant, faithful? Paul says that if we bear one another's burdens we fulfill the law of Christ (Gal 6:2). What do you experience, believe, teach the next generation about law? Discuss, not to convince others but to hear your group work out for yourselves the relationship between grace and law, faith and freedom.

■ What apostolic work have you done in the past? We tend to call apostolate (our being sent) "ministry," another word for service. What would you name as your ministry within the Christian community? What is your ministry to the secular world? Would you want your present ministry recognized by the community in a formal way (a commissioning service or even an ordination)? Why or why not? What future needs of the Church do you envision? What gifts do you have which could fill those needs? What do you envision your future ministry to be? Discuss.

For Further Reading

Beare, Frank. *St. Paul and His Letters*. New York: Abingdon Press, 1962.

Blenkinsopp, Joseph. *Jesus Is Lord: Paul's Life in Christ*. New York: Paulist, 1965.

Paul's Letters
to the Corinthians

10. Paul's Letters to the Corinthians

As we come to the conclusion of our pilgrimage through Scripture, it is appropriate that we study Paul's letters to the Corinthian community. The center of our Christian belief is that Jesus who died was raised to life. In a variety of ways, Paul sets forth in these letters the mystery of faith—that Christ has died, Christ is risen and Christ not only will come again but remains active in his mission and ministry through his body, the Church. In the First Letter to the Corinthians we will pay attention to what underpins Paul's theology—the cross and resurrection; through the paschal mystery, that is, the dying and rising of Jesus, we are united as community and gifted for the community. In Paul's Second Letter to the Corinthians we will see how Jesus' death and resurrection challenges us to compassion and to transformation. Because the dying and rising of Jesus brought about our reconciliation, we are commissioned to be God's ambassadors of reconciliation. Finally, we will turn to the person of Paul himself, accused by so many of us as arrogant, but self-accused as a weakling through whom God's power can operate.

Cross, Resurrection and Community

Paul always maintained that the resurrection of Jesus was crucial to Christianity. "If Christ is not risen, then our faith is in vain" (1 Cor 15:14). It made no difference to him that he had never met Jesus face to face, in the flesh, that he had never met the historical Jesus. Paul's experience, first on the road to Damascus, was an experience of the risen Christ, the Lord. In Chapter 15 of his First Letter to the Corinthians, he explains as best anyone can how Jesus' resurrection signals the triumph of us all over death. Because some of the community at Corinth were so ecstatic about this good news of resurrection, Paul had to remind them that intimately linked with resurrection is crucifixion. Jesus' bloody death on a cross was sheer stupidity to the Greeks, a real stumbling block to the Jews. Yet God brought victory out of a most humiliating, painful situation.

What flows from Jesus' death and resurrection is a new community. John the evangelist would portray this new community at the cross when Mary and John were given to each other (Jn 19); Luke would have the Spirit form the new community for the sake of mission (Acts 1—2). Paul understands that when Jesus' death and resurrection are proclaimed, when we eat his body and drink his blood, we who are many are united as one (1 Cor 10—11). It is Jesus' body and blood handed over which calls us to hand ourselves over to each other.

The community which Paul founded at Corinth, however, was not committed to each other. When they came together to celebrate the Lord's supper and proclaim the Lord's death and resurrection, some came drunk, some came stingy with their pot-luck contribution. Instead of being eager to share their meal with the poor of the community, each one was gorging himself or herself and so insulting the body of Christ, the Church who is the poor. "You eat and drink condemnation of yourselves" (1 Cor 11:29). Although the Corinthians may have used the sacred elements of bread and wine, their supper ritual was not Eucharist because Eucharist calls us to justice and love. Then in a way different from John the evangelist, in a way much more specific, Paul spells out how we should love the body of Christ, the Church. The greediness and competition among community members could be healed if they would recognize that in their community were a variety of gifts, services and works, but all centered in and flowing from the Spirit and all given for the common good (1 Cor 12:4–7). Of all the gifts, of course, the greatest is love (1 Cor 13).

A Share in the Cross and Resurrection

Paul's Second Letter to the Corinthians is probably composed of a few letters, even a fragment that just doesn't seem to fit. Nonetheless, this message was handed down through the centuries not to stimulate the students of ancient manuscripts but "for our salvation." This letter, again so centered in Jesus' death and resurrection, reveals quite a bit about Paul's own share in the Lord's paschal (death and resurrection) experience.

As Paul opens the letter, he is deeply afflicted. He finds in his pain, however, not only God's comfort, but a new sensitivity and compassion toward all who suffer (2 Cor 1:3–7). Some of his suffering is disappointment with the community. He wavers between defensiveness and vulnerability, yet he always exalts God's power at work in him (2 Cor 3:4–6 and again in Chapter 12). God's power expresses itself in the transformation of the Christian. It is the Spirit who is also Lord who leads us to freedom and from glory to glory (2 Cor 3:17–18).

Paul's experience, even in the face of the most terrible difficulties, detailed in Chapter 4 and again in Chapter 11, is freedom. He knows that he carries a treasure in his fragile, rough, earthenware self. He knows that if he carries the dying of Jesus in this broken, beaten and exhausted body of his, the power of Jesus' new and risen life also shines through his flesh (2 Cor 4:10–12).

The newness of the Lord's risen life has brought a new quality of life into this world. Paul calls each of us a new creation (2 Cor 5:17). What has caused this radical newness? Reconciliation has happened through the death and resurrection of Jesus. There is no more alienation between God and us. Barriers are broken. Right relationships are restored. We are no longer strangers to each other but brothers and sisters who are entrusted by God to proclaim the good news of reconciliation (2 Cor 5:18–21). Paul certainly practiced what he preached, trying to break down barriers between races, classes and sexes. "In Christ there is neither Gentile nor Jew, slave nor free, male nor female" (Gal 3:28). He had a more difficult task however with enemies in the mission field, the Judaizers of Galatians and the "super apostles" described in 2 Corinthians, particularly in the last four chapters. In these chapters Paul admits his various weaknesses and seems to boast of his strengths, but he always returns to the praise of God's power, not his own. In fact, his experience is that when he is weakest he comes across the best because God's power can take over his prayer and life and work (2 Cor 12:1–10). All he will boast of is his weakness. Again, in this, he is united with the dying and rising of Christ.

For he was crucified in weakness but lives by the power

of God. For we are weak . . . but in dealing with you we shall live with him by the power of God (2 Cor 13:4).

Guided Prayer

I would suggest that when you take a period for prayer you begin by asking the Spirit to pray within you (for his prayer is perfect praise) and to show you all his gifts to you throughout your life. Ask him to convince you that you are special in the eyes of God, that your gifts are unique, and are needed for the building up of the whole Church-community.

1 Corinthians 1:21-25; 2:1-5:
Look for a while at a crucifix. Is this foolishness? Is it weakness? How do you feel? Is it difficult to think of Jesus crucified? Why? Why not? Are you angry? Afraid? Depressed? Grateful? Wondering? (Remember: there are no wrong ways to feel, or no emotions that are holier than others.) Talk over these feelings with Jesus. Read the passage and respond.

1 Corinthians 12:1-31:
Ask the Lord to reveal what gifts you have (not necessarily those from Paul's list) that are given you for the building up of the body (your family, your community, your neighborhood, your country).

1 Corinthians 12:4-11:
Think of someone you know who has a particular gift mentioned. How do you feel about that person? Tell the Spirit how proud you are of that person, or how jealous. Keep asking him (every day) to show you what your gifts are (probably many not mentioned here). We can't do all the good we would like to do in our lifetime—but our brothers

and sisters all over the world are doing a variety of good works, building up the body. If we "welcome" them (accept, understand, appreciate their gifts and their ministry) we receive their reward (cf Mt 10:40–41).

2 Corinthians 5:16—6:2:

Only if we know how much we lack peace and unity in our hearts, our families, our country, can we appreciate what being reconciled means. Ask Jesus to show you where in your own heart or in your relationships you need reconciliation. Then read the passage and respond to him.

2 Corinthians 3:12-18; return to vv 17-18:

How has the Spirit influenced you through your study of Scripture and your efforts at prayer? How has he transformed you? How do you feel? Tell him what more you want.

2 Corinthians 1:3-7:

Ask Jesus to help you remember difficult situations in the past month. Did your living through those difficulties in any way lead you to grow in compassion for others? Ask to have the heart of Christ so that you may comfort others in their sufferings. Pray for some of those who are suffering now.

2 Corinthians 4:7-11:

How are the things you suffer like Jesus' agony and passion? When in the past has the life and resurrection joy of Jesus sprung from those very difficulties? Ask for the power of his resurrection to become apparent in your life today.

2 Corinthians 12:1-10:

The Lord's power is the theme of this section. When have you seen his power at work in your weakness, frustration, hardships, even in being misunderstood or "persecuted"? After looking at your life with Jesus, narrow it down to just this week's setbacks. Ask him to be strong in your weakness.

Reread 2 Corinthians 12:1-10:

Ask the Lord to reveal times in your life when you were weak but his power was strong.

Exercises

■ This exercise is a reflection on the people in our life whom we call friends and community and thus Church. Draw a circle, two inches in diameter. Then draw another around it, then a third and a fourth circle. In the center circle list those people whom you would consider intimates, those whom you can completely trust. In the next circle list your friends, those with whom you have close bonds of affection. In the third circle, write the names of your companions, people you enjoy being with, those with whom you have a working relationship, perhaps some of your neighbors, your car pool or softball team. The outermost circle is for your acquaintances—or at least some of them. You need not show your circles to anyone, but in your group discuss what Christian community means, what Church means. Is your community different from your family? your parish? Is your Church smaller, closer than the diocese, the parish? Could friends and intimates who are not the same religious denomination be Church for you? Why or why not? Remember, the purpose of this discussion is to clarify our own values about Church and to learn from others' viewpoints. It is not *our* responsibility to convince anyone of his or her errors, not to prove our point. The Spirit can teach, can "guide into all truth" when we keep our minds open and don't argue our version of truth.

■ Open to 1 Corinthians 13, the famous hymn of love. Have someone read it aloud once. Keep the passage open for reference. Take the various specific descriptions of love and apply them to your group. If, for example, Jim, John, Joan, Jean, and Joe are your group, someone might call out, "Jean is not puffed up." "Joe is never rude." "John is not boastful." Leave a quiet moment between these brief affirmations that, indeed, we love well. Conclude with a prayer of thanksgiving for the gift of loving well, your own gift and that of others. This activity will work well in a family too.

■ Another time your group might compose your own hymn of love, listing concrete and contemporary ways to love well. At a later meeting, if you can have the hymn duplicated, you might again apply certain lines to individual members.

■ Read 1 Corinthians 11:17–22 aloud. Celebrate a community supper in your group, but not as the unkind Corinthians did. Arrange for a pot-luck or covered dish dinner for the next meeting. Provide bread and wine. At the next meeting, open with the Our Father as a prayer of reconciliation. Then share the food, eat the bread, drink the wine (or grape juice, if anyone perfers it), talking and laughing as you normally would. When the main dish is finished ask one person to take some bread and wine. Let him or her raise it up, while another person reads 1 Corinthians 11:23–26. Serve dessert. At the end of the evening ask someone to bless the group, and close with a kiss of peace. At the next meeting, share how you felt about this community supper. Where was Jesus in it?

■ By now your group should know each other quite well. This exercise asks you to celebrate the gifts of one another. You might like to set it in the context of a prayer service. Take a sheet of paper for each member of the group. In silence, look at someone and remember his or her gifts shared in this group or gifts you've observed in other situations. List these gifts under the member's name and begin a new sheet for the second person, etc. Collect all papers for John in one pile, Jean in another, etc. Then give the list of John's gifts to Jean, Jean's gifts to Joe, etc. Let the list of gifts be read slowly, reverently, so that Joe is really proclaiming Jean's gifts publicly. At the end of the proclamation, give the lists to their owners.

For Further Reading

Duffy, Regis. *Real Presence*. San Francisco: Harper and Row, 1982.

This book emphasizes how seriously committed we must be to celebrate Eucharist. The author particularly throws light on the Corinthian celebration. He also relates various sacraments to the adult life cycle.

McDonnell, Rea. "Forgiveness and Reconciliation," *New Catholic World*, March/April 1983, pp. 52–54.

Conclusion

We are at the end of our pilgrimage on paper. Thank you for sharing it with me. I only wish I could have geared the prayer and exercises more individually to you. However, the Spirit continues to teach us. The pilgrimage too continues. The risen Christ continues his mission and ministry in the world through us. He is our pioneer (Heb 12:1–2).

Pioneers cut through the underbrush, blaze the trail, forge into wilderness, break into newness. Jesus is our pioneer and he has done all that. With our eyes fixed on Jesus, we are urged to throw off every burden to which we cling and run the race after him (Heb 12:1–2). Like Jesus before us, we are prophets chosen to speak God's word of comfort or challenge. We are to be God's disciples, listening to and learning from him. We are missioned by God, sent surely to our families and communities, but sent also to the suffering and outcast people. We are apostles if we have experienced that Jesus is risen, alive, life-giving. We are God's agents, his ambassadors of reconciliation.

We have work to do. Yet, the work God wants is that we believe in Jesus (Jn 6:29). To believe is to cling, to be united with. I say more: to believe is to embody Jesus. According to Pius XII, we the Church *are* Jesus Christ prolonged in space and time and communicated to humankind. We are the body of Christ, the risen Lord's only means of expressing himself in the world of today. A biblical spirituality is a bodily spirituality. The body politic, the body-Church, and the human body provide the locus for God's activity in history. The body, primarily the body of Jesus but our own bodies too, provides God with a way to express his *hesed* and *emet*. The Word took flesh and is still living among us, in us and through us.

Hopefully we are more at home with the word of God expressed in the Scriptures, more at home with the Word made flesh. If we make his word our home, then we will be his disciples. We will know the truth and the truth will set us free (Jn 8:32). That is his promise and he is faithful. May he continue to bless us all with his *hesed*, his fidelity and his freedom.

For Further Reading

McDonnell, Rea. "Discipleship in the Johannine Community," *New Catholic World*, January/February 1982, pp. 24–27.

McDonnell, Rea. *Sources of Ministry and Mission* (tapes). Canfield, Ohio: Alba House, 1983.